LEADERSHIP STYLE AND EFFECTIVENESS

Examining the Relationship Between Congruency
of Perceived Principal Leadership Style and
Leadership Effectiveness

THE
CORNERSTONE
PUBLISHING

CATHERINE IWUANYANWU-BIEMKPA

Published By:
Cornerstone Publishing
A division of Cornerstone Creativity Group LLC
+1 516-547-4999 | Info@thecornerstonepublishers.com
www.thecornerstonepublishers.com

Author's Information

For speaking engagement, training consulting or to order books by Dr. Catherine Iwuanyanwu-Biemkpa

Please call +1 347-445-9214 or

send email to: catherine.biemkpa@gmail.com

DEDICATION

I would love to dedicate this work to my mother, **Ezinne Juliana Igbeaku Iwuanyanwu**, and my father, **Ezinna Cyril Njoku Iwuanyanwu**, both of the blessed memories. They were and continue to be my greatest sources of academic inspiration. They were both illiterate in their lifetime, but they placed the highest emphasis on education. Mama and Papa, may your gentle souls continue to rest in the Lord! I wish you were both here today to witness this. However, I want you to know that I did not stop because you were no more. It is my heartfelt pleasure to inform you that we did it!

Dedication also goes to my four children: **Eberechukwu, Chioma, Ijeoma, and Uchechukwu.** The sight and thought of them constantly gave me the countless reasons and zeal to keep pushing for greater heights. I continue to unconditionally love you all!

ACKNOWLEDGMENTS

I acknowledge God Almighty for guiding me into and through the process of my doctoral study. I acknowledge and understand that, without God as the leader of my life (CHINEDUM), none of this would be possible. Next, I would like to acknowledge and thank my dissertation committee members, especially the Chair, Dr. David Ferguson, for his advice, kindness, patience, and expertise during this journey. I acknowledge all my pedagogical colleagues at PS 194 in Manhattan, who continuously encouraged and supported my goals of completing my doctoral career. I love you all!

I also, acknowledge all the students and teachers that I taught or supervised. You all gave me the urge to read further in search of deeper knowledge and understanding in teaching and learning. Lastly, I would like to acknowledge and thank all the teachers and principals who took the time to participate in my study. Thank you all, and God bless!

Today, I am a true example that one's socioeconomic status or race does not determine your outcome in life. Through hard work and honest belief in God, your goals can be accomplished. Bravo to me!

ABSTRACT

Despite the constant interest in the theory and practice of leadership as it relates to leadership styles and leadership effectiveness, ongoing debate continues regarding the importance of leadership style and its effectiveness in the administration of underperforming schools. The problem addressed by this study was, despite frequent changes of school leadership, elementary schools in the target school district continue to underperform. The purpose of this study was to investigate the relationship between the congruency of perceived principal leadership style based on the perceptions of teachers and leadership effectiveness in three underperforming public elementary schools in an urban school district. Quantitative methodology and a correlational design were used for the study. The Multifactor Leadership Questionnaire was used for data collection. The participants were the principals and teachers in three elementary schools.

Three research questions guided the study. The result

for question one was that congruency was found between the principals' self-identified leadership style, transformational, and teachers' perceptions of their principal's leadership style. Question two determined the principal effectiveness rating for each study site. Question three's result indicated a strong positive and statistically significant relationship between teacher perceptions of their principal's leadership style and the principal's effectiveness. The results of the study could be used to maintain consistency in transformational leadership behavior and more consistency in the tenure of principals at the target schools. The positive relationship between leadership style and effectiveness should also be viewed as a positive built upon for improvement of the schools. A recommendation for future research is that a study on the same topic be carried out with a larger sample that might be more representative of the population. It is also recommended that a future research is done at higher performing schools to see if similar results would be obtained.

CONTENTS

INTRODUCTION

Much has been contributed to the study of leadership styles. The job of a school leader is a challenging one (Yavuz, 2010). The school leader is charged with the responsibility of hiring teachers and assessing on-the-job performance (Ingle, Rutledge, & Bishop, 2011). Decisions the school leader makes in his or her position affect the welfare of the students and that of the teachers as well as other stakeholders of the school community (Al-Omari, 2013; Ingle et al., 2011). In their practices, school administrators prioritize and focus their actions under challenging conditions, making quality leadership development a requirement for quality principalship (Eyal & Roth, 2011; Piggot-Irvine & Youngs, 2011; Viviane, Robinson, & Le Fevre, 2011).

Although recent qualitative and quantitative analyses have revealed sound program delivery, curriculum coherence, high relevance to stakeholders, and good rates of principal appointments (Hallinger, 2011; Piggot-Irvine & Youngs, 2011), there is a gap between theories of leadership, motivation, and results (Eyal & Roth, 2011). It is obvious that, when many educational leaders lead, it seems like nothing is working (Lowman & Thomas, 2015; Roberson, 2015). The question arises that many leaders, in their zeal to lead using the textbook methods, may fail to recognize the unique nature of each organization and subsequently fail to apply the personalized solutions that take into account the size, technological requirements, environment, and nature of the organization (McKinney, Labat, Myron, & Labat, 2015; Mokhber, Ismail, & Vakilbashi, 2015; Mulford et al., 2009).

Recent studies have investigated, determined, examined, and sought to understand and discover the relationship between leadership styles and leadership effectiveness (Akpan & Archibong, 2012; Brauckmann & Pashiardis, 2011; Döş & Savaş, 2015; Eisele, Grohnert, Beausaert, & Segers, 2013; Eliophotou, 2014; Eyal & Roth, 2011; Ghosh, Satyawadi, Joshi, & Shadman, 2013; Mokhber et al., 2015; Muijs, 2011; Notgrass, 2014; Saeed, Almas, Anis-ul-Haq, & Niazi, 2014). In his study of the relationship between transformational leadership, perceived leader effectiveness and teachers' job satisfaction, Eliophotou (2014) found that teachers' perceptions of leader effectiveness and teachers' overall job satisfaction were significantly linked to the leadership behaviors included in the full range model of leadership. However, Eliophotou recommended further research on investigating the effects of transformational leadership in Cyprus as it relates to both the country's small size and because of the more highly centralized nature of its educational system in comparison to most European and Western countries.

In a validation study of the leadership styles of a holistic leadership theoretical framework, five robust underlying dimensions of practiced leadership styles were identified across the seven participating European countries as instructional, participative, personnel development, entrepreneurial, and structuring (Brauckmann & Pashiardis, 2011). Seeing that the concept of leadership is more than the sum of its constituent parts, Brauckmann and Pashiardis (2011) recommended further research for the essence of leadership as a construct. Additionally, Muijs (2011), in his study of leadership and organizational performance, found that leadership had an indirect impact on student outcomes, even though the role of contingency and school context in shaping leadership is of utmost importance. Muijs recommended a more rigorous quantitative and further qualitative research for measuring impacts and exploring processes that recognize the complexity of schools as organization, as well as avoiding an overly prescriptive approach that limits good practice.

BACKGROUND

The purpose of a school building is to house and protect individuals who are involved in the business of teaching and learning. The main concern of every school is to ensure the maximization of all students' academic achievement (Green, 2012, 2013; Gupta & Singh, 2013). In his compilation of theories of educational leadership, Green (2013) argued that, when a school leader is well organized, has a plan of action that has been developed with the cooperation of the faculty, and implements that plan using a fair process, the end results tend to be goal attainment and high faculty morale.

Unfortunately, leadership styles and leadership effectiveness of principals seem to be affecting the effective running of the public elementary schools in a targeted school district for this study. Based on the data from the district's geography map (New York City Department of Education, 2015), the 15 public elementary schools of the district scored between C and F on both progress report and students' performance.

There is quick succession of leadership in most of the schools because the schools are consistently labeled struggling schools. Most teachers are discouraged on the job because of unfavorable ratings of their job performances based on the Annual Professional

Performance Review, and parents are disappointed, dissatisfied, and frustrated while students continue to underperform (New York City Department of Education, 2015). As a result, the relationship among teachers, administrators, parents, and students continues to adversely affect the rate at which the students attend school and sustain their efforts to learn (Viviane et al., 2011). Also, teachers' motivation and well-being continue to be adversely affected, thereby leading to burnout and low-job performance (Eyal & Roth, 2011).

STATEMENT OF THE PROBLEM

There is a need for school organizations to have effective leaders to properly administer the affairs of the schools (Abdullah & Kassim, 2011; Adeyemo, Dzever, & Lambert, 2015; Akpan & Archibong, 2012). Schools are searching for ways to improve student learning and achievement (Bowers & White, 2014; Bruggencate, Luyten, Scheerens, & Sleegers, 2012; Day, Gu, & Sammons, 2016; Grissom, Kalogrides, & Loeb, 2014; Hardman, 2011; Reza, 2014; Santamaría, 2014; Sun, 2015; Sun & Leithwood, 2015; Tschannen-Moran & Gareis, 2015), and that includes, among other things, replacement of school leadership staff (Arnold, Connelly, Walsh, & Martin-Ginis, 2015; Bipp & Kleingeld, 2011; Döş, & Savaş, 2015; Giles &

Richard, 2012; Notgrass, 2014; Sciarappa & Mason, 2014). The problem of interest for this study was that, despite frequent changes of school leadership, elementary schools in the target school district continue to underperform.

Based on data from the study's target school district, all three of the target elementary schools for this study scored between a C and an F during the 2011-2012 school year on both school progress reports and student performance (New York City Department of Education, 2015). In addition, each of the target schools has changed principals multiple times over the last 10 years (New York City Department of Education, 2015). One example of continued school underperformance despite leadership change for one of the target schools took place between the 2011-2012 and 2012-2013 school years. In 2011-2012, the school had only 17% of students proficient in literacy and 25% in mathematics. This poor student performance prompted a principal change. In 2012-2013, with a new principal, the school had only 3% of students proficient in both literacy and mathematics. Despite the leadership change, the school continued to underperform and actually the student achievement with the new principal was much lower. In addition, despite frequent leadership changes, most teachers are discouraged on the job because of unfavorable ratings of their job performance based on the Annual Professional Performance Review. Data indicate that parents are frustrated, and students continue to underperform (New York City Department of Education, 2015). The proposed study will provide information that could be helpful in addressing the problem of schools continuing to underperform despite frequent changes of school leadership.

PURPOSE OF THE STUDY

The purpose of this quantitative correlational study was to investigate the relationship between the congruency of perceived principal leadership style based on the perceptions of principals and teachers and leadership effectiveness. The independent or predictor variable was leadership style congruency as determined by the correlation between principal perceptions of their leadership style and teacher perceptions of the principal's leadership style. The dependent or criterion variable was leadership effectiveness. Data for measuring each variable were obtained utilizing the Multifactor Leadership Questionnaire (MLQ). The setting for the study included three underperforming elementary schools in an urban school district in New York. The participants were the principals and teachers in the three schools.

The MLQ was administered via email to the three

principals and the teachers in the three schools. Participant responses on the MLQ provided data for calculating the leadership style congruency correlation between principal and teacher responses, as well as leadership effectiveness. The goal was to determine any statistically significant relationship between the congruency of perceived principal leadership style based on the perceptions of principals and teachers and leadership effectiveness. A correlational design was used because it allows the researcher to investigate and determine prevalence relationships among variables and forecast events from current data and knowledge (Curtis & Comiskey, 2015).

Although there are many studies of educational leadership, more studies are required in order to better understand leadership styles of administrators who are charged with the duties of managing already underperforming schools (Eyal & Roth, 2011; Ghosh et al., 2013; Goolamally & Ahmed, 2014; Reza, 2014). There is a need for every organization to determine if the program for developing the leadership styles of its administrators is doing an effective job at producing effective leaders to administer the affairs of the school buildings (Brauckmann & Pashiardis, 2011; Hallinger, 2011; Hui- Wen, Mu-Shang, & Nelson, 2010; Muijs, 2011). This study will address this need for additional research and provide information to address the problem that, despite frequent changes of leadership, elementary schools in the target school district continue to underperform. Information relative to relationships between leadership styles and effectiveness can be helpful in making principal employment decisions for positions in underperforming schools.

RESEARCH QUESTIONS

Research has shown that traditional leadership qualities, such as vision, intelligence, and persistence required of an effective leader, are not always enough to make a leader an effective one (Lowman & Thomas, 2015; Roberson, 2015). The research questions for this study are designed to provide more information relative to relationships that may be important for effective leadership in underperforming schools.

Q1. What is the congruency between principals' perception of their leadership style and teachers' perception of the principals' leadership style in three underperforming elementary schools in an urban New York school district?

Q2. What is the leadership effectiveness level for principals in three underperforming schools in an urban New York school district?

Q3. What is the statistical significance, if any, in the relationship between the teachers' perceptions of the principals' self-identified leadership style and leadership effectiveness level in three underperforming schools in an urban New York school district? The null hypothesis for the third research question states that there is no statistically significant relationship between the correlation values for leadership style congruency based on principals' perceptions of their leadership style and teachers' perceptions of the principals' leadership style and leadership effectiveness level in three underperforming schools in an urban New York school district. The alternative hypothesis states that there is a statistically significant relationship between the correlation values for leadership style congruency based on principals' perceptions of their leadership style and teachers' perceptions of the principals' leadership style and leadership effectiveness level in three underperforming schools in an urban New York school district.

NATURE OF THE STUDY

The study employed a nonexperimental quantitative methodology with a correlation design. In this study, the researcher investigated the relationship between the congruency of perceived principal leadership style based on the perceptions of principals and teachers, the predictor variable, and leadership effectiveness, the criterion variable. The quantitative data for this study were collected through the MLQ responses of the participants. Quantitative methods were used because they allow for a statistical analysis that focuses on available quantitative data as the information relates to the degree of numeric relationships between or among variables (Lim et al., 2014; Thompson, 2015; Trahan & Olivier, 2014). The design for the study was correlation. Correlation design was used because it allows the researcher to study the relationships between and among available facts that are being sought and subsequently, interpreted (Wang, Chen, Xue, & Kang, 2015). This design also allowed the researcher to identify the variables and study relationships among variables in a natural setting (Chiu, 2012; Curtis & Comiskey, 2015; Sabin, 2015). Because the data for the study were numerical quantitative data and the study involved an examination of the relationship between variables, a quantitative method with a correlation design was most appropriate for the study.

The three research questions were designed to provide answers that would be used to achieve the study's purpose. The answer to Research Question 1 provided the values for the variable of congruency of perceptions regarding leadership style at each of the three schools. The answer to Research Question 2 provided the values for the variable of leadership effectiveness at each of the three schools. The answers to Research Questions 1 and 2 provided the values needed to answer Research Question 3 examining the relationship between congruency of perceptions for leadership style and leadership effectiveness, which would achieve the study's purpose.

SIGNIFICANCE OF THE STUDY

The researcher addressed an existing gap in the research by investigating the relationship between the congruency of perceived principal leadership style based on the perceptions of principals and teachers and leadership effectiveness. The investigation utilized a correlation design. The incorporation of correlational design protocol into this research would determine prevalence of relationships among variables, which enables forecasting of events from current data and knowledge (Curtis & Comiskey, 2015).

Therefore, a significance of this research is that the information produced can be used in the forecasting of events related to the study's variables, which will be helpful to school administrators in making decisions.

Achieving the study's purpose would provide information that can be applied to principal hiring decisions and may impact the problem of schools continuing to underperform despite frequent changes in school leadership. This information should help in addressing the challenges of effectively running the targeted underperforming public elementary schools with a particular reference to the leadership styles and leadership effectiveness of the administrators of the schools.

DEFINITION OF KEY TERMS

The following terms are defined for the purpose of this study.

Academic achievement. Academic achievement or academic performance is the outcome of learning. It is the extent to which a student, teacher or a school has achieved their educational goals (Phan, 2012; Tran & Sangalang, 2016).

Congruency. Congruency is the process of finding a match between opposing images or perceptions (Claiborne & Sirgy, 2015; Han & Hyun, 2013).

Effective school. An effective school is one with an optimum learning environment in which students' cognitive, affective, psychomotor, social and aesthetic development are optimally ensured (Döş & Savaş, 2015).

Emotional leadership. This term refers to leadership consisting of different leadership functions found in the literature, including individualized consideration (transformational leadership), providing encouragement and recognition (in both transformational and instructional leadership), presence or visibility (mentioned in instructional leadership and change management), and showing empathy, as in change management and emotional intelligence (Barrett, 2010; Bills, Cook, & Giles, 2015; Brinia, 2011; Foo & Ho, 2012).

Failing public elementary schools. This term refers to schools that fail to achieve adequate yearly progress, which indicates the minimum percentage of students who must be proficient in reading and mathematics for a school to meet the federal standards for the year based on the No Child Left Behind Act (New York City Department of Education, 2015).

Leadership. Leadership is "a process whereby an individual influences a group of individuals to achieve a common goal" (Northouse, 2015, p. 6). Leadership was described by Eyal and Roth (2011) as the ability to enlist, mobilize, and motivate others to apply their abilities and resources to a given cause.

Leadership effectiveness. Leadership effectiveness refers to a leader's ability to build and work with teams that are motivated to set and achieve challenging goals as perceived by subordinates, be it a male or female leader (Brouer, Douglas, Treadway, & Ferris, 2013;

Davis & Stroink, 2016; Kajs & McCollum, 2009; McCarthy & Hammond, 2013; McCollum & Kajs, 2009; Paustian-Underdahl, Walker, & Woehr, 2014).

Leadership effectiveness outcomes. Leadership effectiveness outcomes are measured with a set of MLQ items that determine how a leader is perceived as being effective and creates satisfaction among subordinates. The three leadership outcomes measured by these items include "extra effort" (EE), which refers to elevating the desire for the followers to succeed; "effectiveness" (EFF), which refers to a leader who meets organizational needs and leads the subordinates effectively; and "satisfaction" (SAT), which refers to the leader who uses satisfying methods of leadership style as perceived by the subordinate (Avolio, 1999; Avolio & Bass, 2004; Bass, 1990, 1998).

Leadership practices. This term refers to the five dimensions of model the way, inspire a shared vision, challenge the process, enable others to act, and encourage the heart (Kouzes & Posner, 2008). Bouchamma (2012) operationalized leadership practices as establishing goals and expectations, strategic resourcing, planning, coordination, and evaluation of teaching and the curriculum, promoting and participating in teacher development, and ensuring order and support.

Leadership skills. This term refers to the performance-based traits, characteristics, and competencies that a school administrator must continuously demonstrate for the whole school improvement process, which further refers to leadership attributes such as administrative, interpersonal, and conceptual skills (Agezo, 2010; Kurland, Peretz, & Hertz-Lazarowitz, 2010; Northouse, 2015; Schulte, Slate, & Onwuegbuzie, 2010; Yost, Vogel, & Rosenberg, 2009).

Leadership styles. This term refers to the process by which an individual influences the thoughts and actions of another's behavior (Adeyemo et al., 2015; Al- Omari, 2013; Ibrahim & Heuer, 2016; Northouse, 2015; Oredein, 2010; Paine, Jankowski, & Sandage, 2016). Leadership styles include transformational, transactional, and laissez-faire or passive-avoidant (Bass & Avolio, 1990).

Multifactor Leadership Questionnaire (MLQ). This term refers to a survey instrument used to gather quantitative data. This instrument provides data on self- perception of the school leaders as well as how followers rate their leaders (Avolio & Bass, 1995). A study of transformational leadership with an open-ended questionnaire (Bass & Avolio, 1993) led to the development of the MLQ. The MLQ instrument includes 45 items, 36 of which measure leadership behaviors of principals as perceived by their

28

teachers, while nine items measure skills at motivation and effectiveness in working with others, otherwise known as extra effort, effectiveness, and satisfaction (Eliophotou, 2014).

New York State Standardized Test. The New York State Standardized Test is given annually to students in language arts, math, and science and used to determine school and student achievement (New York City Department of Education, 2015).

School administration. School administration is the act of creating effective learning-teaching and social environment to increase students' and teachers' motivation (Döş & Savaş, 2015). It is the preparation of educational environment of school in a physical area and preparing educational materials while creating an appropriate working environment (Berrett, Murphy, & Sullivan, 2012).

School principal. This term will be interchangeably used with school administrator to refer to the educational leader of the public elementary school responsible for supervising and managing school policies and regulations for insuring staff and students' safe teaching and learning environment (Clifford, Behrstock-Sherrant, & Fetters, 2012; Richards, Aguilera, Murakami, & Weiland, 2014).

Student achievement. Student achievement is a

measure of performance defined as a student's score on the English language arts, mathematics, and science standardized tests (New York City Department of Education, 2015).

SUMMARY

The purpose of the study was to investigate the relationship between the congruency of perceived principal leadership style based on the perceptions of principals and teachers and leadership effectiveness. The method for the study was quantitative. The design was correlational. The participants included the principals and teachers of the targeted underperforming schools. Data were collected using the participants' MLQ responses. The data analysis involved calculating the leadership style congruency correlation between principal and teacher responses as well as leadership effectiveness, which was determined through descriptive statistical analysis. The analyzed data were used to answer the study's research questions, to achieve the purpose of the study, and to address the research problem that, despite frequent changes of leadership, elementary schools in the target school district continue to underperform.

Chapter 1

LITERATURE REVIEW

The purpose of this quantitative correlational study was to investigate the relationship between the congruency of perceived principal leadership style based on the perceptions of principals and teachers and leadership effectiveness. Recent studies on the issue of leadership claimed that an individual's potential for mastering the skills of self- awareness, self-management, social awareness, and relationship management, and translating it into on-the-job success (Goleman, 2011) are not enough to make a leader an effective one (Batool, 2013; Boyatzis, Gaskin, & Wei, 2015; Goleman, 2011; Lowman & Thomas, 2015; Roberson, 2015; Vaida & Opre, 2014; Vivek & Sulphey, 2014). Also, in the context of personality, health, and well-being (Batool, 2013), a leader's social awareness simply means that he or she has the potential to learn or become skilled at the competencies needed to handle a customer or an employee.

A school principal's leadership style is of paramount importance to educational processes (Hauserman & Stick, 2013) and so he or she strives to be very effective in running a school building. Several research studies have been conducted over the past few years to assess, investigate, examine, or explore leadership style based on the competencies associated with intellectual, managerial, and emotional differences (Galvin, Gibbs, Sullivan, & Williams, 2014; Hess & Bacigalupo, 2013; Ugoani, Amu, & Kalu, 2015). The discourse of this literature review will be the examination of the concepts of educational leadership, leadership styles, school culture and climate, emotional competence, leadership effectiveness, school administrator effectiveness, failing schools, self-perception, subordinate perception, congruency studies, and a summary.

DOCUMENTATION

Relevant information for this review of literature was identified through searches for peer-reviewed scholarly publications conducted using various electronic search engines in public and university libraries, which includes Northcentral University's library. Google Scholar and many other online databases were utilized, such as PsychTest, ProQuest, Sage Journals Online, Wikipedia,

EBSCOhost, ERIC, Science Direct, Google.com, and many more. Government-published documents both at the state and federal departments of education websites were also searched. The following key phrases were inputted for the search: educational leadership, leadership styles, leadership effectiveness, organizational culture and climate, failing schools, emotional competence, leadership effectiveness, school administrator effectiveness, self-perception, subordinate perception, and congruency studies.

EDUCATIONAL LEADERSHIP

A main concern of every school is to ensure the maximization of students' academic achievement (Green, 2012, 2013; Gupta & Singh, 2013). Green (2013) argued that, when a school leader is well organized, has a plan of action, and implements that plan, the end result tends to be goal attainment. Green described educational leadership as the process of enlisting and guiding the talents and energies of teachers, pupils, and parents toward achieving common educational aims. Educational leadership is a term generally applied to school administrations that strive to create positive change in educational policy and processes (Avolio, Walumbwa, & Weber, 2009; Brauckmann & Pashiardis, 2011). Brauckmann and Pashiardis (2011) argued that various stakeholders have widened their expectations from school principals demanding higher academic results and performance standards. Educational leadership, therefore, embodies any individual in the school who has a decision-making role and may include the superintendent, assistant superintendents, building principals, assistant principals, and curriculum directors to mention a few.

Educational leadership has been conceptualized as a relationship between educational leaders, instructional staff, and students intended to create opportunities for the exploration and the sharing of knowledge, influencing real changes about the value of lifelong learning, and creating strategies designed to build and promote a shared vision (Batenburg, van Walbeek, & der Maur, 2013; Brauckmann & Pashiardis, 2011; Hauserman & Stick, 2013). Batenburg et al. (2013) believed that creating diversity of roles within teams automatically leads to better performance. Their study found no relationship between team role diversity and team performance, nor that team leader role is related to team performance. However, results also indicated that creating diversity roles within teams may not always lead to better team performance, but rather, team performance should be measured by indicators such as the level of in-team collaboration or collective motivation.

The field of educational leadership continues to be

of paramount interest to researchers. In their review of research topics and methods that comprised the literature on educational leadership and management, Hallinger and Chen (2015) concluded that Asian scholarship in educational leadership and management remains in the early stages of development. In response to scholars' call for a more concerted effort to develop an empirically grounded literature on educational leadership, Hallinger and Chen carried out a review of the research topics and methods that characterize the literature on educational leadership and management in Asia between 1995 and 2012. They found that scholarly interest in different topics have continued to wax and wane across the 18-year period.

However, they observed significant growth in scholarly interest in studying leadership in K-12 schools, school change, effects and improvement, and organizational behavior in education. Ideologies in educational leadership and administration have been explored to determine how they influence the understanding and practice in the field covering a broad range of topics in ethics, governance, diversity, and power (Eacott & Evers, 2016; Samier, 2016). Ethically, the field of educational leadership continues to develop conflict in terms of its relationship to politics, economy, and culture in a democratic society, as well as in terms of professional moral practice as it relates to power and influence (Rodriguez, Martinez, & Valle, 2015; Uljens, 2015).

Uljens (2015) presented that educational leadership is a distributed system from all angles to embrace the interconnection of all professions and institutional practices that will shed more light on any question about ways educational leaders cooperate, learn and lend help across the levels of leadership. He further enumerated a nonhierarchical position to how school and society are related:

School prepares individuals for an existing world, although it does so in a problematizing, non-affirmative fashion, not confirming to the present state of affairs.

Democratic ideals are defended: Education prepares individuals for participation in societal political practices and change.

Human freedom is assumed from provocation (intervention) to self-activity.

The question of the good life remains an open question.

A relative degree of freedom is guaranteed for the state, district, principal, teacher and ultimately for the student.

Uljens' study substantiated the concerns of Rodriguez

et al. (2015), who argued that educational leaders face some challenges in providing the Latino community (the fastest growing demographic in the United States) with rich and equitable education. Using the existing research and theory of educational leadership, Rodriguez et al. established the concept of Latino Educational Leadership to complement the notion that the field of educational leadership draws connections to serve diverse populations.

Among all the educational leadership theories compiled by Green (2013), three stood out in relation to the topic of this study:

Leaders should be servants, coaching, influencing, and empowering subordinates to participate in building learning communities.

If the behavior of the leader places fear in the school, a barrier to effective communication will occur. It is extremely difficult to have a high level of quality in the organization when people are afraid.

Leaders of today's schools should spend time encouraging individuals and groups and helping them to keep up with the changes and demands of the organization so they might understand the benefits to be derived from achieving the school's vision. These three selected educational leadership theories will be referred to as follows: leader as servant, leader as one whose behavior incites fear and distrust, and leader as the instructional leader.

A leader as a servant theory develops leaders who believe that power and authority are for helping others grow (Auxier, 2013; Boyum, 2012; Diehl, 2015; Furrow, 2015; Meyer, 2013; Rohm, 2013). According to Furrow (2015), servant leadership emphasizes shared values, vision, and development resulting in high follower motivation, satisfaction, and retention. Many recent studies have examined, investigated, evaluated, and tried to understand the relationship between servant leadership and job satisfaction (Boyum, 2012; Furrow, 2015; Jordan, 2015). Overwhelmingly, servant leadership has been shown to be a highly effective leadership style that increases job satisfaction in several types of organizations. The results from these studies have indicated that a strong positive correlation exists between servant leadership and job satisfaction in the organization. A leader as a servant also focuses on the followers and the achievement of organizational objectives as a subordinate outcome (Enderle, 2014).

In a study that examined the servant leadership perceptions and practices of active Illinois principals, Enderle (2014) argued that it is of great value that principals adopt leadership practices that contribute to the success of their schools. Analysis of data indicated that Illinois principals are likely to perceive themselves as servant leaders, capable of demonstrating practices that align to the servant leadership construct. This goes to support the leadership skill of a servant leader who is able to serve his or her subordinate by coaching, influencing, and empowering them to participate in building learning communities (Green, 2013). While the principles, values, and practices of servant leadership to teaching are highly valuable to the learning experience of both students and teachers, care should be taken to avoid command and control that might promote dependence, compliance, and passivity (Boateng, 2012; Hays, 2008). The major purpose of servant leadership is to promote flexibility, initiative, responsibility, ownership, self-direction, creativity, empowerment, teamwork and collaboration.

A very critical educational leadership theory is the one where the behavior of the leader places fear in the school because a barrier to effective communication will occur. Sometimes the behavior is easily misread due to the way the leader carries on with his or her daily running of the school. Most teachers become afraid of the leader and spend most of their time in looking for ways of legally protecting their jobs instead of performing high quality job. When this happens, there is lack of empowered work environments (Gupta & Singh, 2013; Lenka & Kant, 2012). Theoretically, therefore, it is extremely difficult to have a high level of quality in the organization when people are afraid. This is compared to a leader's supportive behavior that influences subordinate's creativity and encourages trust between the leader and subordinate (Chen, Yien, & Huang, 2011; Cheung & Wong, 2011). They found that leader support behavior and trust in management enhance employee creativity in an organization (school). Applicably, the principal's leadership behavior changed from inciting fear among the teachers to significantly supportive behavior when our school was listed as a school in need of improvement. She became a transformational leader after she took intensive personality training as part of intervention strategies to save the school from being phased out.

The first day our new principal addressed the staff, she did it on an experience chart, starting with an operational objective well stated, stimulation of prior knowledge, practice activity, and evaluation. This was her way of leading by example: being an instructional leader. Ever since Bush's No Child Left Behind and Obama's Race to the Top (College and Career Readiness), there has been the craze for instructional changes that would move the schools forward and close the academic gap between the economically advantaged and economically disadvantaged students. There has also been the use of three comprehensive school reform programs, which has organized schools for instructional change (Rowan & Miller, 2007) that will enable failing schools to meet up with the challenges. These three programs include Accelerated Schools Project, America's Choice, and Success for All (Rowan & Miller, 2007).

The Accelerated Schools Project uses a system of cultural control to produce instructional change, Success for All uses procedural control, and America's Choice uses professional control. The principal implemented the three programs, which made standardized differences that produced instructional change in the school. In effort to promote leaders as instructional leaders, the instructional leadership institute was designed to explore and increase participants' level of awareness about the importance of analyzing and interpreting data to make more informed decisions about instructional improvement and curriculum alignment for their teachers as well as other elements of leadership training (Smith & Addison, 2013). It is also an effort to place leaders of instruction as principal in schools rather than, placing principals first before they learn to become instructional leaders (Smith & Addison, 2013).

The leaders of today's schools should spend time encouraging individuals and groups and helping them to keep up with the changes and demands of the organizations so they might understand the benefits to be derived from achieving the school's vision. Green (2012) stated, "The leadership of schools has to be distributed, and that means school leaders must have the type of disposition that will influence stakeholders to commit to goal attainment" (p. 1). Most schools in the public system perform poorly in meeting the state-mandated standards. This deficiency has been a matter of concern to all involved, including the federal government, hence the signing of No Child Left Behind Act of 2001 into law by President Bush in January 2002 and President Obama's Race to the Top (College and Career Readiness).

Nationally, educational achievement has been tied to ability to pass standardized tests mostly in English language arts and mathematics. Statistically, most schools in New York State in general and New York City in particular have continuously failed to measure up to standard as evident in their standardized tests performances. The overwhelming number of underachieving schools and students labeled as underachievers across the nation has placed school leadership under scrutiny thereby, leading to frequent replacement of principals in schools that continue to fail in maximizing students' academic achievement. Green (2012) stated, "School leaders and teachers must be of one mind set, congruent in their values and beliefs regarding the development of curriculum and subsequent instruction that meets the needs of each student" (p. 1).

School leaders must, therefore, demonstrate their qualities as instructional leaders of the pedagogical best practices. In his editorial on practices, processes, and procedures for effective school leadership, Green (2012) pointed out essential principles and standards that must be established in order for schools to develop and achieve goals for effectiveness. He also enumerated things that should be in place in order to produce an effective leader, such as a licensure framework of what school leaders need to know and be able to do, ability to build a professional learning community, and ability to implement proven instructional practices with the purpose of addressing the needs of students.

LEADERSHIP STYLES

The growing need for effectiveness and efficiency in leadership has been and continues to be a desired demand from leaders, managers, and administrators of all organizational establishments all over the world (Adeyemo et al., 2015; Al-Omari, 2013; Brauckmann & Pashiardis, 2011; Vermeeren, Kuipers, & Steijn, 2014). This demand is important because it results in employees' attraction and motivation to perform effectively for organizational productivity (Chhabra & Sharma, 2014; Duyar, Gumus, & Mehmet, 2013;

Eisele et al., 2013). Duyar et al. (2013) found that some select aspects of principal leadership and teacher collaborative practices significantly predict teachers' self-efficacy and job satisfaction at, within, and across schools. To this effect, leadership styles come into play.

In the work of Dulewicz and Higgs (2005), they rightly theorized that certain competencies such as traits, styles, and behaviors are indicators of effective leadership. It has been argued that systematic research on the link between transformational leadership and educational outcomes remains limited (Eliophotou, 2014). For this reason, Eliophotou (2014) carried out a study to investigate the link between transformational, transactional, and passive-avoidant leadership behaviors, teachers' perceptions of leader effectiveness and teachers' job satisfaction. The Eliophotou study also examined the conceptual model underlying the scales of the MLQ as the widely used instrument in research on transformational leadership. It was revealed that teachers' perception of leader effectiveness and teachers' overall job satisfaction significantly linked to the leadership behaviors included in the full range model of leadership.

Leadership styles as measured by the MLQ include transformational, transactional and passive-avoidant (Bass & Avolio, 1990). Transformational leadership style refers to the ability of the leaders to cater to the needs of their subordinates or followers and subsequently lead them to effective and productive work performance aimed at organizational productivity. The five underlying dimensional factors of transformational leadership (Hauserman & Stick, 2013; Hunt & Fitzgerald, 2013) are idealized influence (behavior), idealized influence (attribute), inspirational motivation, individualized consideration, and intellectual stimulation. Transactional leadership style, on the other hand, refers to an exchange process (Hauserman & Stick, 2013), and it includes contingent rewards and management by exception (active) and management by exception (passive) as its underlying dimensional factors. The passive-avoidant leadership style, as the name suggests, is seldom discussed because not many leaders can be identified by the style. It is reactive in nature such that the leader only acts when there is a problem. This leader also prefers to delay making decisions or delegates others with responsibilities.

The leadership underlying dimension is that of a leader being absent when needed referred to as passive-avoidant.

Both transformational and transactional leadership styles have been found to have positive influences and outcomes on organizational performances (Hauserman & Stick, 2013; Saeed et al., 2014; Zeb, Saeed, Ullah,

& Rabi, 2015). In a study to examine the relationship between leadership styles and conflict management styles among managers, while handling interpersonal conflict, Saeed et al. (2014) argued that leadership styles or behaviors remain stable over time and are expected to be related to conflict management styles. Analysis of the study data showed that transformational leaders adopted an integrating and obliging style of conflict management, transactional leaders adopted a compromising style, and laissez-faire leaders adopted an avoiding style of conflict management with their subordinates. However, Hauserman and Stick (2013) pointed out that there must be the presence of some transactional leadership characteristics for the transformational leadership attributes to emerge. In a study that examined teacher perceptions of transformational leadership qualities among principals, Hauserman and Stick, using data generated from teachers' MLQ responses, found that teachers strongly preferred behaviors that aligned with the aspects of transformational leadership.

However, transformational and transactional have been viewed as two leadership styles that augment each other (Bass & Avolio, 2000; Hauserman & Stick, 2013). This means that elements of both transformational and transactional leadership qualities are present in effective leaders based on the prevailing circumstances

(Bass, 1985; Belonio, 2012).

Many studies have found that leadership effectiveness is strongly linked to leadership styles, specifically transformational leadership style (Badri-Harun, Zainol, Amar, & Shaari, 2016; Cheok & O'Higgins, 2013; Henkel, 2016; Jayakody & Gamage, 2015; Mokhber et al., 2015). Of these three leadership styles, studies have revealed high favorability for the transformational leadership style for leadership effectiveness (Balyer, 2012; Day et al., 2016; Hunt & Fitzgerald, 2013; Mokhber et al., 2015; Onorato, 2013), with the exception of Ho, Ang, and Tee (2015) who found that transactional leadership influences institutional corporate social responsibility practices more than the transformational style.

In a study to expand the understanding of the relationship between transformational leadership and organizational innovation at the organizational level, Mokhber et al. (2015) argued that organizations are facing a dynamic environment with rapid changes in technologies and high demand for new products and services and companies must develop new and inimitable approaches to attract and retain their customers. The analysis of data from the study questionnaires revealed that there was a positive impact of transformational leadership on organizational innovation. In their work of how successful leaders combine the practices of transformational and transactional leadership in different ways across different phases of their schools' development in order to progressively shape and layer the improvement culture in improving students' outcomes, Day et al. (2016), supported by Hallinger, Wang, and Chen (2013), concluded that successful leaders combine transformational and transactional leadership to both directly and indirectly achieve their leadership effectiveness. This goes to support the notion that most effective leaders integrate four or more of the six identified styles of commanding, visionary, affiliative, democratic, pacesetting, and coaching (Boyatzis, Goleman, & Rhee, 2000) regularly by switching to the one most appropriate in a given leadership situation (Goleman, 2011).

Many recent studies have favored transformational leadership style as a more effective leadership style when compared to transactional and laissez-faire leadership style (Arnold et al., 2015; Henkel, 2016; Ricard, Klijn, Lewis, & Ysa, 2015; Zeb et al., 2015). However, Ho et al. (2015) strongly argued that transactional style influences institutional corporate social responsibility practices aimed at increasing organizational profitability and survival. Transactional leaders possess the qualification of maintaining the status quo by adhering to the prescribed management guidelines. They are usually not risk takers. They focus on efficiency, control, stability, and predictability while working within the boundaries set by the organization. The dictates of the transactional leadership domains often leads to followers' dissatisfaction and burnout (Sonnino, 2016). Transformational leadership mostly comes after transactional in order to remedy the dissatisfaction and burnout created by the excessive exertion of the transactional style.

The transformational leader, therefore, is the one who raises his followers to "higher levels of motivation, making changes and shaping the future" (Sonnino, 2016, p. 19). School Culture and Climate Studies abound that have pointed out the effect of school culture and climate in school effectiveness and improvement. These studies argue that the leader's leadership style and emotional competence might not be enough (Lowman & Thomas, 2015; Roberson, 2015) to make a difference in school improvement, but a combination of the leader's instructional leadership, strong influence of development orientation, teachers' sense of collective efficacy, and overall organizational commitment lead to positive school culture and climate (Balyer, 2012; Bowers & White, 2014; Bruggencate et al., 2012; Bulach, Boothe, & Pickett, 2006; Calik, Sezgin, Kavgaci, & Cagatay, 2012; Day et al., 2016; Furman, 2012; Grissom et al., 2014; Hallinger & Murphy, 2013; Hallinger et al., 2013; John & Taylor,

2014; Neumerski, 2013; Runhaar, Konnermann, & Sanders, 2013; Santamaría, 2014; Spillane & Kim, 2012; Spillane, Kim, & Frank, 2012; Urick, 2016).

Bulach et al. (2006) found that principals use certain behaviors, such as trust, openness, listening, and caring attitude, while supervising their subordinates. They argued that the use or failure to use these behaviors creates the type of leadership style that could positively or negatively affect the climate and learning environment in any educational setting. Balyer (2012) argued that, transformationally, school principals frame their attitudes to help them move their schools forward. In his study to discover the level of transformational leadership behaviors principals demonstrate during their daily administrative practices, Balyer found that school principals demonstrate a high level of characteristics aligned with transformational leadership behaviors. In a study to examine the relationships between school principals' instructional leadership behaviors and teachers' collective- and self-efficacy, Calik et al. (2012) found that instructional leadership had a significant direct and positive impact on collective teacher efficacy.

It is evident that, to make an effective workplace or effective school, leaders should endeavor to work toward making happy teachers who would eventually make happy students that would become achieving students (Abdullah & Kassim, 2011; Adeyemo et al., 2015; Asmawi, Rahim, & Zainuddin, 2015). In a study to explore the practice of instructional leadership among principals based on four dimensions of defining and establishing school goals, managing the instructional program, promoting the learning environment, and creating a friendly and cooperative school environment, Abdullah and Kassim (2011) found that the school organization needs to have an effective leader to properly administer changes at the school level in order to move in line with the current global changes. The analyzed data from the study revealed that principals practiced a high level of defining and establishing school goals among other responsibilities. It was also revealed that the principals possessed positive attitude towards organizational change in the three dimensions of cognitive, affective, and behavioral.

Additionally, Adeyemo et al. (2015) argued that emotional intelligence and leadership styles play important roles in the quality of employees' work life, and so in their study to investigate the effects of organizational climate, leadership style and emotional intelligence on the quality of work life, Adeyemo et al. found that the combination of the three variables of organizational climate, leadership style, and emotional intelligence was effective in predicting quality of work life while showing leadership style as the most potent predictor. Asmawi et al. (2015) found that both participative leadership and supportive leadership styles have significant positive relationship with both normative and effective commitment. Leadership behavior variables such as order, expectations, and parental involvement make up overall school climate and culture that result in high organizational commitment and eventually predict reduced work stress, lower employee turnover, and high faculty morale (Asmawi et al., 2015; Green, 2013; John & Taylor, 2014).

In his compilation of theories of educational leadership, Green (2013) found that, when a school leader is well organized, has a plan of action that has been developed with the cooperation of the faculty, and implements that plan using a fair process, the end results tend to be goal attainment and high faculty morale. In a study that explored the relationships among principals' leadership style, school climate, and the organizational commitment of teachers, John and Taylor (2014) found that these three variables of principals' leadership style, school climate, and organizational commitment of teachers were interrelated. Most significantly, teachers' commitment was positively related to climate openness of principals' supportive behavior and teacher engagement, intimacy, and lower teacher frustration.

EMOTIONAL COMPETENCE

Emotional competence is required to set a positive tone for organizational productivity. Emotional competence has been operationalized as that capability that prevents a leader from saying an employee is difficult to be led, managed, supervised, or with whom to work. It is the ability to decipher other people in terms of what motivates them, how they work and how to work collaboratively with them (Batool, 2013; Luu, 2013; Vaida & Opre, 2014; Vivek & Sulphey, 2014). In a study that substantiated the interconnections of emotional intelligence, trust, and corporate social responsibility, Luu (2013) argued that corporate governance is built on the responsibility of members towards other stakeholders both within and outside the organization. Data analysis revealed that emotional intelligence is the beginning of the organization's effort towards strong corporate governance.

Batool (2013) argued that emotional intelligence has overwhelmingly become popular as a measure for identifying potentially effective leaders and as a tool for developing effective leadership skills. In a study that explored the relationship between emotional intelligence and effective leadership to evaluate the tendency of emotional control in a gender inclusive working class at a managerial level in both private and public sector, Batool's analysis of the collected data concluded that emotional intelligence can help to reduce stress, improve performance, and sense of achievement by motivating the subordinates within the organization and helps to enhance the productivity of the employees to meet organizational end goals in an ethical way by putting positive impacts on the society as a whole.

In their study of emotional intelligence versus emotional competence, Vaida and Opre (2014) highlighted three main approaches to studying this relationship: emotional traits, emotional abilities, and emotional competence. They maintained that the relationship between emotional intelligence and emotional competence is that of inseparability, even though the concept of emotional competence remains a missing puzzle from the advantages of emotional intelligence. The authors stated, "Emotional intelligence is a prerequisite that forms the building bricks for developing emotional competence which in turn, leads to performance" (Vaida & Opre, 2014, p. 31). Recent studies have found that people with well-developed emotional competence deliver greater profits to their organizations, and success in business has been attributed to effective use of emotional competence (Vivek & Sulphey, 2014). While emotional intelligence is viewed as a set of innate factors, emotional competence can be learned and developed

(Boyatzis et al., 2015; Goleman, 2011; Vivek & Sulphey, 2014).

Many research studies have been conducted to explore, examine, determine, and investigate the impact of the three leadership styles in the workplace (Abdelhafiz, Alloubani, & Almatari, 2015; Belonio, 2012; Jiang, 2014; Pillay, Viviers, & Mayer, 2013; Sehrawat & Sharma, 2014; Sonnino, 2016; VanderPal, 2014; Yusof, Kadir, & Mahfar, 2014), and it has been widely acclaimed that job satisfaction, organizational engagement, and followers' motivation are positively related to the extent to which a leader can put his or her emotions into good use (Hess & Bacigalupo, 2013). Yusof et al. (2014) maintained that the combination of cognitive and emotional abilities leads to desirable decision making because their findings showed that emotional intelligence is essential for successful leadership as it provides many benefits to leaders.

In a study to determine whether emotional intelligence can predict an effective leadership, Pillay et al (2013) found positive correlations between self-reported emotional intelligence and transformational leadership. However, negative correlations were found between emotional intelligence and laissez-faire leadership as well as differences between specific demographic variables. Sehrawat and Sharma (2014) maintained that positive job performance depends on the emotional intelligence of both leaders and followers. In determining the effect of leadership styles on employee job satisfaction and the effect of employee job satisfaction on employee job performance, Belonio (2012) found, among other things, that transformational, transactional, and laissez-faire leadership styles have a positive effect on various aspects of employee job satisfaction. Employee job satisfaction had positive effect on job performance. The study finally concluded that leaders and managers combine the various leadership styles in proportions that produce a positive result in the administration of their leadership daily duties.

Effective leaders, therefore, use their emotional intelligence to effectively manage themselves, others, and their organization (Arnold et al., 2015; Batool, 2013; Caruso & Salovey, 2004; Esposito, Freda, & Bosco, 2015; Eyal & Roth, 2011; Goleman, 2011;

Hui-Wen et al., 2010; McKinney et al., 2015; Mokhber et al., 2015; Posthuma, 2012; Singh, 2013; Urtasun & Nuñez, 2012; Viviane et al., 2011; Zembylas, 2010). In a study that investigated the potential impact of leadership style on leaders' emotional regulation strategies and burnout, Arnold et al. (2015) hypothesized that the relationships existed between leadership styles, emotion regulation, and burnout. Results from analyzed data showed that transformational leadership predicted deep acting and genuine emotion, contingent reward predicted surface and deep acting, management by exception predicted surface acting while laissez-faire predicted genuine emotion.

Batool (2013), while exploring the relationship between emotional intelligence and effective leadership to evaluate the tendency of emotional control at managerial level, found that the relationship was positive and significant. This means that emotional intelligence is one of the useful tools that helps a leader to judge people more clearly and closely and build a connection between people. Eyal and Roth (2011) found that leadership styles among school principals play a significant role in teachers' motivation and well-being. While trying to identify common personal and professional strategies present in successful principals, McKinney et al. (2015) theorized that the ability of a principal to lead the students of the new millennium is based on his or her ability to set goals of excellence for teachers, students, staff, and themselves. The outcome of analyzed data revealed that there is a reflection of how teachers perceived their principals' leadership traits and behaviors as well as how these behaviors impact teacher morale.

Posthuma (2012) theorized that there was a need to understand how and when the regulation of emotions can facilitate effective conflict management. His study revealed that a broad range of positive and negative emotions, such as anger, enthusiasm, excitement, guilt, and remorse, are significantly related in complex and varied ways to various aspects of conflict management. While investigating whether there is a significant correlation between the emotional intelligence behaviors of leaders and the job satisfaction of their employees, Singh (2013) argued that leaders need to recognize both the interpersonal and intrapersonal emotions of their employees and react appropriately to them based on the leaders' level of emotional intelligence. The research found that there is a significant correlation between the employees' sense of job satisfaction and their leaders' interpersonal and intrapersonal emotional behaviors. These findings would indicate that emotional competence is also required to achieve leadership effectiveness.

LEADERSHIP EFFECTIVENESS

Leadership effectiveness takes more than strong leadership skills. Recent studies have found that leadership effectiveness involves a leader's ability to put in place a team capable of accomplishing the strategic visions and missions of the organization as a matter of priority (Brouer et al., 2013; McCarthy & Hammond, 2013; Paustian-Underdahl et al., 2014). McCarthy and Hammond (2013), while exploring which leadership dimensions predict leadership effectiveness across different rating sources in a public sector organization, revealed that different rating sources value different leadership competencies quite differently. In the same light, it has been perceived that men are more effective as leaders than women. However, Paustian-Underdahl et al. (2014) found that, when all leadership contexts are considered, men and women do not differ in perceived leadership effectiveness. Studies have found and suggested that leadership effectiveness should include the consideration of personality characteristics, political skills, and cross- cultural experiences (Brouer et al., 2013; Caligiuri & Tarique, 2012; Chen & Li, 2013; Goldring, Mavrogordato, & Haynes, 2015; Hamlin, Kim, Chai, Kim, & Jeong, 2016; Lakshman, 2013; Sadeghi & Pihie, 2012; Werchan, Fahey, Anglin, & Keebler, 2016).

Caligiuri and Tarique (2012), supported by Goldring et al. (2015), found that personality characteristics and cross-cultural experiences are some of the competencies that predict supervisors' ratings of global leadership effectiveness. In a study that tested the model that political skill is related to both leader and follower effectiveness through leader-follower relationship quality, Brouer et al. (2013) argued that leader political skill is associated with leader effectiveness and follower effectiveness through relationship quality. Analyzed data upheld the hypotheses by revealing that leader political skill enhances the quality of relationship and positively affects leader and follower effectiveness relationships. In a study that determined heads of academic departments' leadership styles and its relationship with leadership effectiveness, Sadeghi and Pihie (2012) argued that academic departments play an important role in the success of institutions of higher education and the success of the departments depends on effectiveness of their head. Data analysis revealed that lecturers perceived that the heads of departments exhibited combination of the three leadership styles (transformational, transactional and laissez-faire) as measured by the MLQ instrument. Further regression analysis demonstrated that the domains of these leadership styles are significant predictors of leadership effectiveness while specifically pinpointing contingent reward as having important effects on leadership effectiveness.

Chen and Li (2013) concentrated on spiritual leadership effectiveness which they linked to determinants such as follower's self-concepts, culture, and managerial position. It was revealed that culture differs on the spiritual leadership effectiveness while managerial position plays no significant role between motivational factor of spiritual leadership and role performance. According to Avolio et al. (2009), spiritual leadership is acknowledged as a more value-oriented and new-genre leadership theory. The construct of spiritual leadership is also viewed as rooted in an intrinsic motivation model incorporating vision, hope or faith, and altruistic love to portray an effective leader (Fry, 2003). The spiritual leadership draws on the values, attitudes, and behaviors of leaders that motivate self and others through spiritual well-being that encourages followers' ability to experience meaning in their lives as employees. Lakshman (2013) argued that attributional patterns and variations across cultures are crucial and called for cross- cultural leadership effectiveness to be adequately addressed.

Numerous recent studies have verified, explored, addressed, investigated, examined, identified, and presented that, of the three leadership styles measured by the MLQ instrument, transformational leadership style is a high and positive predictor of leadership effectiveness in any organization (Eliophotou, 2014; Goolamally & Ahmad, 2014; Hallinger, 2011; Jarrett, Wasonga, & Murphy, 2010; Kuran, 2013; McKinney et al., 2015; Petridou, Nicolaidou, & Williams, 2014; Sciarappa & Mason, 2014; Tschannen-Moran & Gareis, 2015; Wu, 2014). In a study that investigated the link between transformational, transactional, and passive-avoidant leadership behaviors, teachers' perceptions of leader effectiveness, and teachers' job satisfaction, Eliophotou (2014) argued that systematic research on the link between transformational leadership and educational outcomes remains limited. Data collected and analyzed revealed that teachers' perceptions of leader effectiveness and teachers' overall job satisfaction significantly were linked to the leadership behaviors included in the full range model of leadership.

Similarly, Goolamally and Ahmad (2014) argued that leadership concept remains surrounded by ambiguity and remains difficult to distinguish between leaders and non- leaders as well as between effective and ineffective leaders. In their study that sought to identify and affirm the conceptual framework and attribute of school leaders (principals) needed to achieve leadership sustainability and school excellence, they found that there were five important traits or attributes which a school leader or principal must possess in order to make a school an excellent one (integrity, forward looking, inspirational, competent, and self-efficacy). Hallinger (2011) also argued that the exponents of a given position have neither defined sharply what is signified by the concept of instructional leadership nor made their assumptions explicit. In his study that presented a research- based model leadership for learning, he found that significant progress has been made in identifying the means by which leadership impacts on learning. However, Hallinger recommended a future research to focus on contextualizing the types of leadership strategies and practices discussed in this study such as: the need to obtain better information not just about what works but what works in different settings and contexts.

Still in the same line of thought, Jarrett et al. (2010) theorized that many schools still reflect the factory model of management and it is no longer sufficient for schools to meet the needs of all students as once stipulated in No Child Left Behind. In their study that examined teacher perceptions of the practice of co-creating leadership and its potential impacts on student achievement, they found that teachers in high-performing schools scored significantly higher on perceptions of the practice of co-creating leadership dispositional values and the presence of institutional conditions that facilitate the practice. This is a valuable construct needed to enhance leadership effectiveness.

In a study that addressed the importance of storytelling in the 21st-century business context where the emphasis has shifted from the trainer to the learner, from the producer to the consumer, and from the leader to the follower, Kuran (2013) argued that the use of the human side and the ancient tool of storytelling rather than a theoretical approach would lead to inspirational leadership. Utilizing a combination of the author's practical insight on storytelling and real-life storyteller leaders as a study methodology,

Kuran concluded that storytelling skill supports leaders in their communication and, consequently, suggested that leadership communication should focus on both the content and the context of the message. It was further recommended that leaders should endeavor to excel at the art of becoming a skilful storyteller.

In their effort to identify common personal and professional strategies present in successful principals who lead National Blue Ribbon schools, McKinney et al. (2015) found that there is a reflection of how teachers perceived their principals' leadership traits and behaviors as well as how these behaviors impact teacher morale. The finding is in line with past literature on principal leadership, teacher morale, and school climate and culture, in which the morale of the teacher, in turn, impacts the level of instruction delivered to students. This is another valuable variable needed for effective leadership that can make a school an excellent one. Petridou et al. (2014) argued that evidence of research and studies of efficacy are weak in the field of educational leadership when compared to other various fields.

In their study to develop and validate a new School Leaders' Self-Efficacy scale, an instrument designed to measure school leaders' self- efficacy, which might be used in the context of professional development activities for school leaders, in particular, or in studies of school leadership in general, Petridou et al. found an eight-factor structure of creating an appropriate organizational structure, leading and managing the learning organization, school self-evaluation for school improvement, developing a positive climate and managing conflicts, evaluating classroom practices, adhering to community and policy demands, monitoring learning, and leadership of continuing professional development. This study is important because it developed a scale, analyzed and evaluated the scale, and provided evidence to support the validity and reliability of the scale, all of which can play vital roles in enhancing leadership effectiveness.

Sciarappa and Mason (2014) examined the perceived efficacy of a U.S.-based national principal mentor-training program and found that mentors were well prepared, good listeners, and instrumental in strengthening their instructional leadership. It was also found that the program was critical to the adjustment and success of the new principals in their first year of leadership assignment. In their position that schools need trustworthy leaders skillful in cultivating academic press, teacher professionalism, and community engagement in their schools to foster successful student learning, Tschannen-Moran and Gareis (2015) explored the relationships among faculty trust in the principal, principal leadership behaviors, school climate, and student achievement. Results from analyzed data showed that faculty trust in the principal was related to perceptions of collegial and instructional leadership, as well as to factors of school climate such as teacher professionalism, academic press, and community engagement.

A well-led organization is one in which tasks are transacted efficiently. For leadership effectiveness to occur in an organization, shared visions and missions are well articulated by the leaders and other stakeholders, with the leaders creating a work environment that encourage creative thinking, designing and implementing new and cutting edge program that challenges the status quo (Abdullah & Kassim, 2011; Adeyemo et al., 2015; Agezo, 2010; Akpan & Archibong, 2012). Therefore, there is need for school administrator effectiveness for the administration of the underperforming public elementary schools.

SCHOOL ADMINISTRATOR EFFECTIVENESS

Leaders are the designers of organizational behaviors, and, at schools, the most important individual charged with the responsibility of conducting and overseeing teaching, learning, and other daily activities is the school administrator (Akpan & Archibong, 2012; Anderson & Macri, 2009; Berrett et al., 2012; Döş & Savaş, 2015; Gülcan, 2012; Samier & Atkins, 2010;

Yavuz, 2010). Gülcan (2012) carried out a study to determine whether a school principal's instructional competencies are dependent upon the type of school or the principal's specialization. The study outcome provided data used in making decisions on how to select and educate school principals for their job.

Akpan and Archibong (2012) believed that the ability of the school administrator to perform his or her leadership role effectively could be influenced by the way he or she perceived himself or herself, so they investigated the predictive effect of personality factors of self-concept, self-esteem, self-efficacy, and locus of control on instructional and motivational leadership role performance effectiveness of secondary school administrators.

The collected and analyzed data showed that the four personality variables as mentioned above significantly predict instructional leadership role performance effectiveness of school administrators as well as predict their motivational leadership role performance effectiveness, when combined. In a study that examined school district administrators' discourse around student learning in the context of provincial curriculum and student performance standards and accountability systems, Anderson and Macri (2009) argued that there is need for a multidimensional agenda for student learning in public education. The analyzed data identified six core frames at play in the superintendents' discourse on students learning: measurable academic achievement, personalized preparation for postsecondary destinations, a well- rounded education, personal development, faith- or values-based education, and social identity development and a broader frame of developing the whole child. The school district administrative discourse around student learning is a variable that is needed to determine leadership effectiveness of the school district administrators that transcends to the school building leadership effectiveness of the principal.

While trying to understand the implementation process of technology integration in a school district from an administrator's perspective, Berrett et al. (2012) argued that innovative technology approaches to learning often meet resistance within schools. The collected and analyzed data revealed that all the administrative informants indicated they understood that they were part of a larger community within the great implementation process. This is a variable that can enhance leadership effectiveness if the leader has the awareness that culture and change are antithetical, and change threatens stability as indicated in past studies. In their study to determine the characteristics and roles of elementary school administrators according to teacher and administrator perspectives, and discuss their training in the context of effective schools, Döş and Savaş (2015) argued that the lack of education received by current managers can lead to serious educational problems and so to establish effective schools, the characteristics expected to be possessed by a school principal must be determined. Collected data were analyzed, and results showed that school principals have a key role in increasing student success by creating effective learning-teaching and social environment and increase students' and teachers' motivation. Also revealed are the characteristics of being good humored, hardworking, and patient.

Samier and Atkins (2010) theorized that positions of power and influence provide motive and opportunity for the damaging character of personality disorder (narcissism) to negatively affect the work life of colleagues and sabotage organizational effectiveness, ranging in degree from mild annoyance to extreme disabling. They examined the problem of destructive narcissism as an aspect of the emotional dimension of educational administration and found that there are four aspects of graduate professional programs examined for the effects of destructive narcissistic pattern: student recruitment, curriculum, narcissistic professors, and research activities. This finding is in line with past literature that shows considerable attention given to the destructive narcissistic pattern as the root cause of a hostile organizational environment.

In a study to investigate the effectiveness of the supervision process conducted by primary education supervisors in the light of the evaluations of school principals, Yavuz (2010) argued that it is no easy task on the part of the principals to measure the degree to which school principals implement their duties because they are required to perform various tasks in different fields. Using the descriptive data analysis, he found that school principals did not have adequate knowledge about the criteria by which they were evaluated, supervisors relied heavily on what could be called document check, and they thought supervisors could not perform the roles of orientating, guiding, and improving teachers' educational behavior satisfactorily. Past literature has shown that principals have responsibilities focused on two roles of educational leadership and school management. The principal participant group in this study reported that they waste time on administrative duties and would rather have a consideration of reduction of bureaucracy in schools.

In a study to identify and affirm the conceptual framework and attributes of school principals needed to achieve leadership sustainability and school excellence, Goolamally and Ahmad (2014) found that there were five important traits or attributes that a school leader or principal must possess in order to make a school excellent: integrity, forward looking, inspirational, competent, and self-efficacy. Also, studies have revealed there is a reflection of how teachers perceived their principals' leadership traits and behaviors as well as how these behaviors impact teacher morale (McKinney et al., 2015; Tschannen-Moran & Gareis, 2015; Wu, 2014), with faculty trust as a significant predictor (Tschannen-Moran & Gareis, 2015). Numerous studies on leadership effectiveness have revealed that educational leadership effectiveness as it relates to school administration is a challenging construct (Chen & Li, 2013; Goldring et al., 2015; Hamlin et al., 2016; Lakshman, 2013; Sinnema, Ludlow, & Robinson, 2016; Werchan et al., 2016), which entails more than being a strong and skilful leader. In their study to determine the relationship between leadership styles and leadership effectiveness of heads of academic departments, Sadeghi and Pihie (2012) found that lecturers perceived the heads of departments exhibited combinations of transformational, transactional, and laissez-faire leadership styles. The analysis from this 2012 study demonstrated that the domains of these leadership styles can be significant predictors of leadership effectiveness.

FAILING SCHOOLS

Most schools in the public system perform poorly in meeting the state-mandated standards (Finnigan, Daly, & Stewart, 2012). In their study to better understand the process through which school staff in underperforming systems diagnose problems, search for solutions, and incorporate those strategies into efforts at reform, Finnigan et al. (2012) found limited evidence of organizational learning. Rather, evidence revealed superficial use of restructuring planning and diagnoses of the root causes of low performance are rarely carried out, leading to limited engagement in staff professional development activities. This deficiency in performance has been a matter of concern to all involved, including the federal government (Gagnon & Mattingly, 2015), which prompted the signing into law of the No Child Left Behind Act of 2001 by President Bush.

Nationally, educational achievement has been tied to ability to pass standardized tests mostly in English language arts and mathematics (Beckett, 2014; Firth, Melia, Bergan, & Whitby, 2014; Gorton, Williams, & Wrigley, 2014; Reyes & Garcia, 2014). Statistically, most schools in New York State in general and New York City in particular have continuously failed to measure up to standards, as evidenced by standardized test performance ("Mayoral Election May Threaten

Progress in NYC Schools," 2014; Mercado, 2012).

Since the passage of No Child Left Behind, the term failing schools is used in conjunction with accountability (Finnigan et al., 2012). This accountability indicates that someone is blamed for the students' low test scores (Agasisti, Bonomi, & Sibiano, 2014; Finnigan et al., 2012). Efficiency is the ability to transform inputs into outputs (Agasisti et al., 2014). In their study of measuring the managerial efficiency of public schools, Agasisti et al. (2014) found that efficiency and educational equity are complementary in primary public schools, with the most efficient school having the lowest internal variance between the students' achievement scores.

Also, most schools seemed to be efficient when the external variables are not considered, because their background favored them. However, they are not efficient based on managerial perspective. With the passage of No Child Left Behind, schools are legally responsible for student performance and are consequently blamed for any kind of poor student performances (Jefferson, 2015; Lisa, Barbour, & Menchaca, 2014; Wang & Decker, 2014). However, with the passage of President Obama's Race to the Top, the blame for poor student performance shifted from school to the teachers (Gagnon & Mattingly, 2015; Pulley & Jackson, 2016), making teachers accountable for failing schools; therefore, the solution to failing schools became the firing of the staff and closing of failing schools.

The issue of failing schools has triggered actions ranging from loss of democratic control by being taken over by the state and turned over to private charter corporations to being put under mayoral control (DeJarnatt, 2013; Nelson-Smith, 2014; Wang & Decker, 2014). However, the failing schools continue to fail. Examples are found in New Jersey, Cleveland, and Chicago, which have been either taken over by the state or placed under mayoral control for over 20 years with no improvement (Finnigan et al., 2012; Pulley & Jackson, 2016). The only exception is with the private charter schools that report improvement only when they exclude the low-performing students' test scores from the overall performance grades of the schools (Finnigan et al., 2012).

The main concern of every school and its administration is to ensure the maximization of the entire students' achievement (Green, 2012, 2013; Gupta & Singh, 2013; Ruebling, Stow, Kayona, & Clarke, 2004). For the failing schools to improve in academics, additional instructional leaders are being sought among the teaching staff to serve as literacy and mathematics coaches in order to augment the efforts of the principals as the instructional leaders, because they (the principals) still have to shoulder the enormous responsibilities of being instructional leaders as well as facing huge management issues in schools (Kent, 2005; Lieberman & Miller, 2005; Stock & Duncan, 2010). However, a controversy and unanswered questions lie in the fact that, at some point the mentors or coaches need to be coached or mentored in some aspect of their expected specialties (Stock & Duncan, 2010).

In their study about who is mentoring the mentors, Stock and Duncan (2010) found that over 50% of the instructional coaches did not have a mentor, and 90% of the respondents agreed that mentoring was important to both beginning and experienced instructional coaches. At the early period of hiring instructional coaches from among the teaching staff to help effectively implement the comprehensive school reform programs in failing schools, these coaches received mentoring in literacy and mathematics, which they turn-keyed to the rest of the teaching staff in the week that followed.

After the first 2 years, the mentoring stopped and the newly hired instructional literacy and mathematics coaches were left to swim and sink on their own. According to this 2010 study, the mentoring program was withdrawn by the school districts. Suffice it to say that, even though an attempt was made to increase the number of instructional leaders by hiring instructional coaches from among the teaching staff, it did not last long because instructional leaders were not mentored on the areas they thought were important to be mentored in due to barriers that hindered the districts from providing a mentoring program (Stock & Duncan, 2010). Principals, as leaders of today's schools, constantly spend time encouraging individuals and groups, helping them to keep up with the changes and demands of the organizations so they might understand the benefits to be derived from achieving the school's vision.

Another controversy related to the topic of failing schools stems from the fact that existing educational leadership preparation programs seem to focus on a lack of contextual relevancy and instructional leadership (Cunningham & Sherman, 2008). This calls for the nature of principal preparation to move beyond acculturation to district norms and irrelevancy to building future leaders' capacity for continuous educational improvement (Cunningham & Sherman, 2008). Also, in their research, Ruebling et al. (2004) suggested that leaders are unable to orchestrate multiple changes that provide opportunities for teachers to work in teams, focus resources effectively on implementing the curriculum, and establish accountability for results.

SELF-PERCEPTION

This study involves a calculation of the correlation between school principals' self-perceptions of their leadership style and teachers' perception of their school principal's leadership style. Therefore, a discussion of the topic of self-perception is presented. Theoretically, through the interpretation of the meaning of one's behavior in the context it occurs, he or she begins to understand own's attitude and preferences as much as they understand those of others (Critcher & Gilovich, 2010). How we convey ourselves before others matters a lot because it goes to show our self-perceptions (Bledow, 2013; Davies, 2015; Hornquist, Rickardsson, Lannering, Gustafsson, & Boman, 2014; Oneal, Odom-Maryon, Postma, Hill, & Butterfield, 2013; Shreck, Gonzalez, Cohen, & Walker, 2014).

A leader's self-perception in relation to his or her subordinates determines the leadership style and leadership behavior of such a leader who, most of the time, strives for subordinates' job satisfaction by maintaining a conducive work environment for organizational productivity (Belonio, 2012; Ealias & George, 2012; Pugno, 2009; Werner, 2013).

According to Werner (2013), the leadership style of a principal is of paramount importance to the success of his or her school. Therefore, the author concluded that servant leadership, when combined with emotional intelligence, is strongly correlated in the leadership of elementary school principals. Furthermore, a study of the congruence of leader self-perceptions and follower perceptions of authentic leadership identified support for the interaction effect of leader self-perceptions and follower perceptions of authentic leadership in predicting job satisfaction, integrating the leader- and follower-centric perspectives of authentic leadership (Černe, Dimovski, Marič, Penger, & Škerlavaj, 2014).

Data from 24 supervisors and 171 followers produced a robust evidence to conclude that authentic leadership is paramount in administration of most organizations since the analysis of the data indicates that follower perceptions of such leadership predicts their job satisfaction. Further analysis of the data revealed and supported the congruence between leader self-perceptions and follower perceptions of authentic leadership is also beneficial and they are needed to be present at high levels for organizational productivity in terms of followers' job satisfaction.

Principals' and teachers' beliefs are indicators of their perceptions and judgments as related to leadership styles and leadership effectiveness (Adeyemo et al., 2015; Al- Omari, 2013; Avolio & Bass, 1995; Döş & Savaş, 2015; Eliophotou, 2014). It is often perceived that the responsibility for a school's success or failure belongs primarily to the principal of that school (Döş & Savaş, 2015). In their study of the administrator's roles in the context of effective schools, Döş and Savaş (2015) found that there is a strong relationship between school administration and student success. A principal's leadership style affects the way he or she leads the subordinates and subsequently contributes to a positive or negative school climate and culture (Abdullah & Kassim, 2011; Adeyemo et al., 2015; Arnold et al., 2015; Eisele et al., 2013). Addressing principals' leadership style, by focusing on the principals' perceptions of their leadership style and the teachers' perceptions of their principals' leadership style, combined with leadership effectiveness, will help to alleviate the challenges of effectively running the underperforming public elementary schools with a particular reference to the leadership style and leadership effectiveness of the administrator of the schools.

This study measured the self-perceived leadership style of principals. It is the perception of transformational leaders that, by adhering to this often motivational leadership style (transformational), they have what it takes to bring out the best in their followers or subordinates (McKinney et al., 2015; Mokhber et al., 2015; Saeed et al., 2014). The MLQ evaluation of the three different leadership styles of transformational, transactional, and passive-avoidant allows the individual leaders to measure how they perceive their specific leadership behaviors with the use of the self-form of the MLQ. This measure was utilized in answering Research Question 1 by determining the relationship between this measure of self-perception and the perceptions of subordinates working as teachers for the leader.

SUBORDINATE PERCEPTION

A review of subordinates' perceptions has invoked the construct of perceived organizational support or the extent to which subordinates believe their leaders or work organizations value their contributions and care about their well-being (Baran, Shanock, & Miller, 2012; Kurtessis et al., 2015). Several recent studies have demonstrated the relationships that exist between perceived organizational support and affective commitment on the part of the organizations' subordinates (Baran et al., 2012; Kurtessis et al., 2015; Shen et al., 2014; Wei & Si, 2013). Through the organizational support theory, it is identified that leadership, employee-organization context, human resource practices, and working conditions determine employee's orientation toward the organization and work, employee performance, and well-being (Kurtessis et al., 2015).

Most studies involving leaders' and subordinates' ratings have revealed higher disagreement between their ratings that are related to lower subordinates' well-being (Barreto, 2013; Giorgi, Leon-Perez, Cupelli, Mucci, & Arcangeli, 2014; Hassan, Wright, & Yukl, 2014; Klaussner, 2014; Skogstad et al., 2015). Giorgi et al. (2014) found that the leaders' capacity to understand subordinates' stress is associated with subordinates' psychological well-being. The subordinates' perceptions could result in either abusive leadership stemming from initial subordinates' perceptions of the leader's injustice, or leader's perceptions of unacceptable subordinate's behavioral response (Klaussner, 2014). Relationships among organizational trust in the leader, leadership behaviors, organizational climate, and productivity play a vital role in the subordinate's perceptions (Reza, 2014; Tschannen-Moran, & Gareis, 2015; Sun, 2015). Tschannen-Moran and Gareis (2015) found that faculty trust in the principal was related to perceptions of collegial and instructional leadership, school climate, as well as student achievement as it correlates with trust, leadership behaviors, and climate.

CONGRUENCY STUDIES

A construct variable for the current study is the congruency relationship between principals' perceptions of their leadership style and teachers' perceptions of the principals' leadership style. Therefore, a thorough review and discussion of congruency studies is important for the study. Studies abound that have pointed out the effect of leader and follower congruence in achieving workplace person-environment fit that leads to quality, trust, employee job satisfaction, commitment, and job performance for organizational productivity (Lewis, 2010; Zhang, Wang, & Shi, 2012). These studies found that the leaders' ability to build teams with actual job performance depends on the leadership's influence on members, teams, and organizations. The leader-member exchange theory affirms that leaders form strong trust, emotional, and respect-based relationships with selected team members (Zhang et al., 2012). This theory posits that leaders do not treat all subordinates the same because the work-related attitudes and behaviors of the subordinates depend on how they are treated by their leaders (Chen, Wen, Peng, & Liu, 2016; Lewis, 2010; Zhang et al., 2012).

Congruency is conceptualized as the process of finding a match between opposing images or perceptions (Claiborne & Sirgy, 2015; Han & Hyun, 2013). Theoretically, the consistency among strategy, structure, and culture enhances organizational performance (Chen et al., 2016; Lin, 2014; Von Schoultz & Wass, 2016), and, subsequently, the different facets of consumer behavior are predicted and explained by self-image congruence (Claiborne & Sirgy, 2015; Hosany & Martin, 2012; Rajaguru & Matanda, 2013).

In a study to understand which strategy-structure and strategy-culture contingencies facilitate superior post-acquisition performance, Lin (2014) concluded that different acquisition strategies require different levels of headquarters centralization and interdivisional integration in the organizational structure, as well as different degrees of acculturation in the organizational culture. Subsequently, because research on workplace loneliness is heavily based on the followers' perceptions, recent studies have been on the perspective of leader-follower congruence (Chen et al., 2016).

In their study to examine how the leader-follower relationship mediates the relationship between leader-follower congruence or incongruence in workplace loneliness and turnover intentions, Chen et al. (2016) found that (a) leader-member exchange was higher when leaders and followers were aligned in terms of workplace loneliness than otherwise; (b) in the case of leader- follower congruence, leader-member exchange rose as the workplace loneliness fell; (c) in the case of incongruence, followers had lower leader-member exchange when they were lonelier than their leaders; and (d) leader-member exchange partially mediated the leader-follower congruence or incongruence effect of workplace loneliness or followers' turnover intention. This study contributed positively to the workplace leaders' congruence with the followers' loneliness at work. In their test of a model that includes self-image congruence, cruise ship passengers' experiences, satisfaction, and behavioral intention, Hosany and Martin (2012) found that self-image congruence affects passengers' experiences but indirectly influences satisfaction levels, and satisfaction in turn, positively relates to respondents' propensity to recommend others.

Also, there is a congruence of a person's interest and the kind of professional career interest (Wille, Tracey, Feys, & De Fruyt, 2014). In a study that investigated Holland interest-occupation congruence across time for a sample of college alumni as tracked for the first third of their professional career, Wille et al. (2014) carried out an examination of congruence in all its complexity that resulted in interest-occupation comparisons that could be related to general and career specific well-being. They found that there is indication of moderate levels of stability in interests and occupations across a 15-year time interval. Congruence analysis also indicated significant interest-occupation fit at the beginning and later of the 15-year career. This study revealed that job change moderated the association between interest-occupation congruence and life satisfaction, leading to a reported higher level of satisfaction with little job change.

In leadership, many recent studies have been carried out to assess, review, examine, explore, test, investigate, and demonstrate the effects and consequences of cross-cultural, family, and gender congruency in an organizational setting (Barnard & Simbhoo, 2014; Dimitrov, 2015; Hernandez-Bark, Escartín, & van Dick, 2014; Liao, Liu, Kwan, & Li, 2015; Monzani, Hernandez-Bark, van Dick, & Peiró, 2015; Mustafa & Lines, 2016; Rowold, 2014; Zeinabadi, 2013). Mustafa and Lines (2016) carried out a comprehensive review of cross-cultural literature focusing on the emergence and effects of culturally congruent leadership and found that gaps existed because studies on cross- cultural leadership have often focused on the measurement and description of relationships without paying adequate attention to addressing the importance of the effects of cultural values across levels, interaction between individual and societal values, and the production and effects of culture-leadership congruity.

Warning that the outcome of Spanish studies on gender and leadership may be quite different from those of the United States and other European countries as a result of their late development of gender equality, Monzani et al. (2014) reviewed the current theoretical and empirical literature on gender and leadership, which focused on four aspects of the underlying mechanism of gender inequality, gender and leadership behavior, the relation of female representation in top management and on boards with organizational performance, and female representation and nonperformance-related organizational outcomes. It was revealed that Spain's current severe economic crisis might provide a chance for gender equality development or trigger a regression toward traditional gender roles in the society. Liao et al. (2015) examined the relationship between ethical leadership as perceived by employees and the family satisfaction of the employees' spouses and found that employees' perceptions of ethical leadership in the workplace positively influenced their spouses' family satisfaction.

Similarly, Barnard and Simbhoo (2014) explored the meaning essence of authenticity as lived in the work-life experiences of senior managers in public service, and found that authenticity is experienced as an affective state that results from a continuous self-appraisal of the extent to which expression of self is congruent with a subjective and socially constructed expectation of self in relation to others, and it (authenticity) seems to develop through a continuous process of internal and external adaptation that leads to building a differentiated but integrated identity of self. In the case of gender and leadership, it has been found that according to the congruity theory, female managers face hard times at work because of the incongruity between female gender and leadership role expectations (Monzani et al., 2015). Due to this incongruity, female leaders hardly perceive themselves as authentic leaders. However, Monzani et al. (2015) hypothesized that authentic leadership dimensions mediate the relation between managers' biological gender and their organizational identification and found that men scored higher on authentic leadership, female managers scored lower in authentic leadership and identified less with the organization; no gender differences were found in the high team prototypicality condition.

In a study that explored the way leadership influences an organization to become humane through its features and behaviors, as well as the organizational circumstances in which humane leadership can be nurtured, Dimitrov (2015) found the following five leadership subthemes: (a) company values for leadership styles and employee treatment, (b) the legacy of one charismatic leader, (c) leader-follower communication, (d) how the workplace feels intrinsically, and (e) how the work environment becomes negative. The study recommended a future research of more culturally diverse organization to establish individualism and collectivism employees' expectations of their leadership would make a difference for the sustenance of a humane organization.

SUMMARY

In this review of literature, the concept of educational leadership has been considered in relation to leadership styles and leadership effectiveness. The review has also briefly conceptualized the three leadership styles as measured by the MLQ. Emotional competence has also been reviewed as a part of the puzzle in the effective utilization of intelligence in decision making processes by administrators. In addition, school climate and culture are discussed as key factors to achieving school effectiveness and improvement. A school administrator's leadership style and leadership effectiveness are pertinent indicators of what is happening to the school's culture, climate, and, most especially, student achievement. Failing schools as a construct are discussed as a predictor to constant changing of the leadership of the target schools in the study.

Self- perception and subordinate perception are discussed to make clear the importance or value of there being a congruency between the leaders' self-perception of their leadership styles and the perception of others (subordinates). Finally, congruency studies as a construct have been discussed to highlight the possible relationship of the correlation or agreement of the leaders' self-perceptions of their leadership behaviors and the followers' perceptions of their leaders' leadership behaviors. These variables may be indicators as to why the school is underperforming or passing. Finally, despite many varied efforts to improve schools, many schools continue to underperform.

Chapter 2

RESEARCH METHOD

The purpose of this quantitative correlational study was to investigate the relationship between the congruency of perceived principal leadership style based on the perceptions of principals and teachers and leadership effectiveness. Chapter 3 begins with the listing of the research questions and hypotheses and review of the variables in the study. The beginning of the chapter is followed by the description of the research method and design of the study that includes the rationale for the selection of the research method and design.

This chapter also includes a discussion of data collection processes and analyses, population, sample, assumptions, as well as a description of the instruments and variables. This chapter will conclude with a description of the limitations, delimitations, ethical assurances and a summary. The research questions for this study were designed to provide more information relative to relationships that may be important for effective leadership in underperforming schools.

Q1. What is the congruency between principals' perception of their leadership style and teachers' perception of the principals' leadership style in three underperforming elementary schools in an urban New York school district?

Q2. What is the leadership effectiveness level for principals in three underperforming schools in an urban New York school district?

Q3. What is the statistical significance, if any, in the relationship between the teachers' perceptions of the principals' self-identified leadership style and leadership effectiveness level in three underperforming schools in an urban New York school district? The null hypothesis for the third research question is that there is no statistically significant relationship between the teachers' perceptions of the principals' self-identified leadership style and leadership effectiveness level in three underperforming schools in an urban New York school district. The alternative hypothesis is that there is a statistically significant relationship between the teachers' perceptions of the principals' self-identified leadership style and leadership effectiveness level in three underperforming schools in an urban New York school district.

RESEARCH METHOD AND DESIGN

This study utilized quantitative methodology. Quantitative methods were used because it allows for a statistical analysis that focuses on available quantitative data as related to the degree of numeric relationships between or among variables (Lim et al., 2014; Thompson, 2015; Trahan & Olivier, 2014). The design for the study was correlation. Correlation design was used because it allowed the researcher to study the relationships between and among available facts that were being sought and subsequently interpreted (Wang et al., 2015). This design allowed the researcher to identify the variables and study relationships among variables in a natural setting (Chiu, 2012; Curtis & Comiskey, 2015; Sabin, 2015). Correlation design provided the opportunity to recognize trends and patterns in data collected to see whether the variables were related, as well as the strength and direction of the relationship between the variables of the phenomenon under study (Creswell, 2009; Curtis & Comiskey, 2015; Yin, 2009). The purpose of the study was to examine the relationship between variables. The specific variables for this study were leadership style of principals based on the congruency of perceptions between principals and teachers and leadership effectiveness. Therefore, correlation design was appropriate for achieving the purpose of this study.

The three research questions were designed to provide answers that were used to achieve the study's purpose. The answer to Research Question 1 provided the value for the variable of congruency of perceptions regarding leadership style. This value served as the independent or predictor variable for the study. The answer to Research Question 2 provided the value for the variable of leadership effectiveness, which was the dependent or criterion variable for the study. The answers to Research Questions 1 and 2 provided the values needed to answer Research Question 3, which achieved the study's purpose.

Achieving the study's purpose provided information that can be applied to principal hiring decisions and may impact the problem of schools continuing to underperform despite frequent changes in school leadership.

POPULATION

The population for the study was all principals and teachers in the three targeted underperforming schools. The three principals were all females. One of the principals was Hispanic, and two were African American. The average number of years of service for the principals at the schools was 2 years. Seventy-eight percent of the teachers had 3 or more years of teaching experience. The average attendance rate of the teachers was 96%. The average racial percentages for the teachers at the targeted schools were as follows: 59.3% African American, 18.5% Hispanic, 11.1% White, and 11.1% Asian. The average gender percentages for the teachers are 11.1% male and 88.9% female.

SAMPLE

The study utilized a sample of convenience. The criteria for participation were being either a principal or a teacher at any of the three targeted schools and the willingness to acknowledge informed consent, complete the MLQ, and submit it. The type of convenience sampling was nonprobability. Nonprobability convenience sampling is a nonrandom method of selecting elements in which not all elements have an equal chance of being selected (Baker et al., 2013). Recent concerns about how time consuming and costly it was to collect and infer data have led most researchers to resort to nonprobability sampling methods that included the convenience method as an alternative means of data collection

(Baker et al., 2013). However, there are advantages and disadvantages of nonprobability convenience sampling (Baker et al., 2013; Hays, Liu, & Kapteyn, 2015; Riley, Hays, Kaplan, & Cella, 2013; Rivers, 2013).

Nonprobability convenience sampling was convenient and relatively easy for collecting data from a known group. It allowed more flexibility and it was less complicated. This method was time saving and less expensive because the samples were familiar to the researcher (Hays et al., 2015; Riley et al., 2013). Nonprobability convenience sampling had the disadvantages that included not being a proportion of the population because it chose the most available samples. Selection depended on the situation and no assurance that each item had a chance of being included as a sample.

There was no accurate means of assessing how well the samples were represented. The results were of limited value and so generalization of the study findings may be restricted (Baker et al., 2013).

INSTRUMENT

The instrument for this study was the MLQ, which was designed by Bernard M. Bass and Bruce J. Avolio (2000) and is distributed by Mind Garden. The development of the MLQ was derived from a study of transformational leadership with an open-ended questionnaire (Bass & Avolio, 1993) that led to the development of the MLQ. The MLQ instrument includes 45 items, 36 of which measure leadership behaviors of principals as perceived by their teachers, nine items that measure skills related to motivation and effectiveness in working with others, otherwise known as extra effort, effectiveness, and satisfaction (Eliophotou, 2014).

The MLQ is an instrument used to evaluate leadership style as well as leadership outcome factors including effectiveness (Hauserman & Stick, 2013). The three different leadership styles evaluated by the MLQ are transformational, transactional, and passive- avoidant (Avolio & Bass, 1995, 2004). Transformational leadership is the first leadership style on the MLQ. It describes a leader who motivates followers to use their confidence toward accomplishing desired outcomes. For this style, five subscales of idealized influence (attribute and behavior), inspirational motivation, intellectual stimulation, and individualized consideration are utilized by the MLQ.

Transactional leadership is the second leadership style measured by the MLQ, and it describes leaders who lead by maintaining the status quo within the structure of organization as they identify the followers' skills and subsequently assign roles and responsibility to accomplish the desired outcomes. For measuring transactional style, the MLQ utilizes two subscales of contingent reward and management by exception-active. The third leadership style measured by the MLQ is passive-avoidant, which describes leaders who choose to delay making decisions or delegate others to act on their behalf.

This style has two identified subscales as laissez-faire and management by exception- passive. This has been shown to be the least effective of the three identified leadership styles. The MLQ also includes three leadership outcome factors of extra effort, effectiveness, and satisfaction (Bass, 1990, 1998).

The researcher obtained permission to use the MLQ instrument for research purposes. The MLQ is available in both self-forms and rater forms. The self-form measures self-perceptions of leadership style based on behaviors. This form was administered to the school principals. The rater form is used to measure leadership style and effectiveness (Bass & Avolio, 2000) and was administered to the teachers. The MLQ is the most widely used instrument for the assessment of the transformational leadership style. It is extensively validated in the manual created by Avolio and Bass. Leading experts in the field of leadership styles in various organizations such as business, education, government, medical, military, and religion heavily rely on the MLQ as a measure to determine effective leadership (Bass & Avolio, 2000).

According to the reports from the MLQ manual, scores for transformational characteristics were found to have reliabilities ranging from .70 to .83 (Avolio & Bass, 2004). Multiple studies by different authors have also substantiated the reliability and validity claims of the instrument (Fiery, 2008; Finley, 2014; Hauserman & Stick, 2013; Omer, 2005). Generally, the MLQ instrument has been extensively studied and found to exhibit internal consistency for test and retest reliability, external predictive validity, and construct validity (Eid et al., 2004). The MLQ instrument was chosen by the researcher over all other instruments because its validity and reliability scores range from moderate to good (Avolio & Bass, 1995, 2004).

OPERATIONAL DEFINITION OF VARIABLES

The variables are principal self-identified leadership style, teacher perception of principal identified leadership style, leadership style congruency, and leadership effectiveness. The principal self-identified leadership style variable was derived from the MLQ responses by the principal participant group. Teacher perception of principal identified leadership style was based on teachers' MLQ responses and was the rating value principals' teachers give for their principal's self-identified leadership style.

Leadership style congruency was the agreement or the correlation between the self- identified leadership style rating from the principal participant group and the teacher participant group's rating of their principals' self-identified leadership style. Leadership effectiveness was derived from the teacher participant group's MLQ responses to the leadership outcomes of effectiveness, extra effort, and satisfaction.

Principal self-identified leadership style. This term refers to the mean rating value for the highest rated leadership style self-identified by each of the three target school principals as determined by each of the three principal's responses to MLQ items measuring leadership style.

Teacher perception of principal identified leadership style. This term refers to the mean rating value for the highest rated leadership style self-identified by each of the three target school principals as determined by each of the three principal's teachers' responses to MLQ items measuring their principal's self-identified leadership style.

Leadership style congruency. This term refers to the comparison between the mean rating values for the highest rated leadership style self-identified by each of the three target school principals and the mean rating value for the highest rated leadership style self-identified by each of the three target school principals as determined by each of the three principal's teachers' responses to MLQ items measuring their principal's self- identified leadership style.

Leadership effectiveness. This term refers to the overall mean rating value for MLQ items measuring leadership effectiveness based on teacher participant group responses for each of the three target school sites.

DATA COLLECTION, PROCESSING, AND ANALYSIS

Permission from the target school district, New York City Department of Education's Institutional Review Board, and Northcentral University's Institutional Review Board were obtained by the researcher. Any additional permission required for the study was also obtained. In addition to protecting the dignity, rights, and welfare of human participants in a research (Cozby & Bates, 2012; De Wet, 2010; Northcentral University, 2010, 2011; Resnik, 2011), Northcentral University's Institutional Review Board requires that "research in which data are collected through the involvement of human participation may not be conducted in the absence of IRB approval" (Northcentral University, 2010, p. 1).

Data collection. Following the written approvals, an email including information about the study was sent to the potential participants (see Appendixes A and B) via the school district email system. This informational communication included contact information for potential participants to use if they had any questions or concerns. Next, an online email was sent via the school district email system and utilized for obtaining informed consent and for administering and collecting the MLQ responses from the participants. No personal identifiers were present on the MLQ. Email addresses used to distribute the MLQ were stored on a password protected computer and any paper documents were also stored in a locked cabinet. Data were organized in a spreadsheet based on the study's variables.

Research Question 1 data analysis. For Research Question 1, data were analyzed for each of the three target schools and three values were determined. First, the composite mean rating value for the highest rated leadership style self-identified by each of the three target school principals as determined by each of the three principal's responses to MLQ items measuring leadership style was calculated. The composite mean value was calculated using values ranging from 0 to 4 for each MLQ item with 0 being the least positive response and 4 being the most positive response. The MLQ items utilized for this step included Items 2,

6, 8, 9,10, 13, 14, 15, 18, 19, 21, 23, 25, 26, 29, 30, 31, 32, 34, and 36 for the transformational leadership style; Items 1, 4, 11, 16, 22, 24, 27, and 35 for the transactional leadership style; and Items 3, 5, 7, 12, 17, 20, 28, and 33 for the passive-avoidant leadership style. Next, the composite mean rating value for the highest rated leadership style self-identified by each of the three target school principals as determined by each of the three principal's teachers' responses to MLQ items measuring their principal's self-identified leadership style were calculated. For this step, the same item numbers aligned with the three leadership styles were utilized. Finally, a comparison between the composite mean rating values for the leadership style self- identified by each of the three target school principals and the teachers' mean rating values for the highest rated leadership style self-identified by each of the three target school principals as determined by each of the three principal's teachers were executed to check for congruency.

Research Question 2 data analysis. Data for Research Question 2 was analyzed using the rating value for effectiveness based on teacher responses to the MLQ items measuring the domains for effectiveness. These items included 37, 40, 43, and 45 for effectiveness; 39, 42, and 44 for extra effort; and 38 and 41 for satisfaction. The data underwent descriptive statistical analysis to provide a composite mean value representing the level of leadership effectiveness as perceived by the teacher participant group at each of the three target school sites. The rating values utilized in the analysis for each MLQ item range from 0 to 4 with 0 being the least positive rating and 4 being the most positive.

Research Question 3 data analysis. For Research Question 3, a Pearson correlation analysis was utilized. For this analysis, the relationship between the teacher rating values for their principal's highest self-rated leadership style and the three leadership effectiveness values found for Research Question 2 were calculated. The results of this analysis were used to make the determination whether to reject or fail to reject the hypotheses for Research Question 3.

ASSUMPTIONS

It was assumed that the convenience sample adequately represented the population. It was assumed that participants submitting the MLQ were willingly participating in the study. It was also assumed that the participants responded to the MLQ items accurately and honestly without prejudice. Another assumption was that the participants' responses to the MLQ reflected their lived experiences at the respective locations of the study.

LIMITATIONS

Several factors may threaten the validity of a study's outcomes based mostly upon the fact that the survey items used in data collection might yield some misleading responses (Arffman, 2015). The threats to validity are both internal and external. Threats to internal validity, which refers to whether the experimental condition makes a difference or not and whether there was sufficient evidence to support the claim, may be limited in terms of some participants not staying through the entire period of the study. The likelihood of some of the principals being replaced before the end of the study was also a limitation. Also, a limitation was that the instrument did not collect any demographic data. Therefore, the researcher cannot be certain that the convenience sample was demographically representative of the population.

A threat to external validity refers to whether the study outcome could be generalizable to a larger population. If not, then it is a limitation. Because the study was done in only one urban school district in New York, which consists of up to 32 school districts, it could not be easily generalizable to other districts or statewide. For feasibility purposes, the number of schools and subsequently the participants was restricted to fewer participants and schools. Another limitation was the simplified criteria to determine participants using a sample of convenience. The results might not be easily generalizable to other districts and populations because of this limitation.

DELIMITATIONS

There were the delimitations of population and sample criteria. This study was delimited to data from only three schools in one urban school district location in New York. The study was also delimited to the criteria of convenience sampling. The study was therefore delimited to just 1 out of 32 school districts which included only three principals and teachers at three schools with voluntary participation from the three underperforming schools targeted for the study as identified in the study problem and purpose.

ETHICAL ASSURANCES

Ethical issues were adhered to during the study. Adherence to protocol that assures that the procedures are focused upon collecting data and not changing people (Northcentral University, 2011; Resnik, 2011) was of utmost importance. The purpose of the study was carefully explained both at the beginning and then during data collection in an accurate and understanding manner through email correspondence. Permission to conduct the study was obtained from the appropriate entities and approval through New York

106

City Department of Education's Institutional Review Board and Northcentral University's Institutional Review Board prior to any data collection. This was in compliance with the federal requirements for ethical research and the protection of human subjects (De Wet, 2010; Resnik, 2011).

SUMMARY

Through this quantitative correlational study, it was possible to investigate the relationship between the congruency of perceived principal leadership style based on the perceptions of principals and teachers and leadership effectiveness of the three targeted underperforming public elementary schools. Using quantitative methodology, the MLQ data were collected from participants through their responses which were used to measure the variables: leadership style, leadership style congruency, and leadership effectiveness. The population for the study consisted of both the principals and teachers of the three targeted schools. The population was selected using the nonprobability convenience sampling. Both the principals' and the teachers' perceptions of the principals' self- identified leadership style and leadership effectiveness were measured using the MLQ tool. The gathered data from the participants' responses was used for both descriptive and inferential statistical analyses to answer the research questions and to make the decisions regarding the hypotheses.

Chapter 3

FINDINGS

The purpose of this quantitative correlational study was to investigate the relationship between the congruency of perceived principal leadership style based on the perceptions of principals and teachers and leadership effectiveness. The Multifactor Leadership Questionnaire (MLQ) was used to collect data for both the principals' and teachers' perceptions of the principals' leadership behaviors and effectiveness. The problem of interest for this study was that, despite frequent changes of school leadership, elementary schools in the target school district continue to underperform.

PARTICIPANT RESULTS

The original proposal for the study called for seven

schools to be study sites. However, only three of the seven school sites were willing to participate. After receiving approvals from both Northcentral University's Institutional Review Board and the Institutional Review Board of New York City Department of Education, the study participants were recruited from the three schools through informational flyers placed in potential participants' mailboxes and email. Follow-up phone calls, visits to the schools, and email contacts were made seeking voluntary participation. The online survey was set up including a page one Informed Consent Form for participants to read and click a 'yes' to consent to the study participation or click a 'no' to opt out of the study. Those who acknowledged their informed consent to participate in the study were linked to the survey instrument.

There were a total of 36 respondents from three different school sites for the study: three principals and 33 teachers. All three principals were female and of the teachers, who responded, 25 were female and eight were male. The average number of years of service for the principals at the participating schools was 2 years. Seventy-eight percent of the teachers had 3 or more years of teaching experience. The average attendance rate of the participating teachers was 96%. Most of the respondents (59.3%) were African American, 18.5% Hispanic, 11.1% White, and 11.1% Asian.

QUESTION 1 RESULTS

Q1. What is the congruency between principals' perception of their leadership style and teachers' perception of the principals' leadership style in three underperforming elementary schools in an urban New York school district?

The MLQ was used to determine the highest rated leadership style for each of the three study site principals based on each of the three principal's responses to MLQ items. Each of the three principals, self-rated "transformational" as their highest rated leadership style. The mean rating for the site one principal for the transformational style was 3.45. The mean rating for the site two principal for transformational style was 3.45. The mean rating by the site three principal for the transformational style was 3.30.

The MLQ responses from teachers at each of the three study sites were used to determine the congruency between teachers' perceptions of their principal's leadership style and the principals' perceptions. The result for question one was that, at all sites, the teachers indicated agreement and congruency with their principal's self-rating by rating "transformational" as their principal's highest rated style. Site one teachers' mean rating for transformation was 2.46. Site two's mean rating was 2.27 and site three's was 2.56. Table

1 illustrates the descriptive statistics for the principal and teacher ratings of the principals' leadership style.

Table 1

Principal and Teacher Mean Ratings for Leadership Style

Site	Transformational		Transactional		Passive-avoidant	
	Principal	Teachers	Principal	Teachers	Principal	Teachers
1	3.45	2.46	1.88	2.27	0.25	1.15
2	3.45	2.27	1.88	2.04	0.75	1.15
3	3.30	2.56	2.88	2.28	0.75	1.25

QUESTION 2 RESULTS

Q2. What is the leadership effectiveness level for principals in three underperforming schools in an urban New York school district?

The MLQ was used to determine the effectiveness mean rating for each of the three study sites' principals based on teachers' responses to MLQ items at each of the three sites. The mean effectiveness rating as determined by teacher responses to MLQ items 37, 40, 43, and 45 included site one 2.50, site two 2.20, and site three 2.60. These mean rating values from teachers at each of the three study sites were used to determine the leadership effectiveness level for

112

the principals in three underperforming schools. The mean effectiveness rating values for each of the three sites represented the results for research question two. Table 2 illustrates the effectiveness mean ratings for the three sites.

Table 2

Effectiveness Mean Rating for Three Study Sites

Site	Effectiveness Rating
1	2.50
2	2.20
3	2.60

QUESTION 3 RESULTS

Q3. What is the statistical significance, if any, in the relationship between the teachers' perceptions of the principals' self-identified leadership style and leadership effectiveness level in three underperforming schools in an urban New York school district?

Research question one and research question two findings were used in the analysis for research question three. Research question one findings indicated congruency between principal MLQ ratings of leadership style and the ratings by each principal's teachers. At all three sites, both the principal and the teachers rated "transformational" as the highest rated principal leadership style, which demonstrated congruency. Teachers' MLQ responses were averaged for each of the three study sites and the mean values for transformational, were used for the predictor variable in the question three correlation analyses.

The results for research question two, which provided the values for the outcome variable, effectiveness, were used in the correlation analysis for question three. A Pearson correlation analysis examined the relationship between each teacher's mean rating of their principal's "transformational" style and their rating of each principal's effectiveness for each of the three study sites. At site one, the teacher ratings for transformational style ranged from 2.05 to 3.75 with a mean rating of 2.46. The site one teacher ratings for principal effectiveness ranged from 1.50 to 4.00 with a mean of 2.50. Appendix C provides the descriptive statistics for leadership style and effectiveness for each teacher respondent at site one.

The Pearson correlation analysis for site one utilized each teacher rater's mean rating for the principal's leadership style and effectiveness to determine the relationship between the two variables and to determine any statistical significance. The inferential analysis revealed a strong positive correlation between the teacher's rating for their principal's leadership style, which was congruent with the principal's self-rating, and the principal's effectiveness ($r = .804$). According to Creswell (2012), an r value between .66 and .85 indicates a strong positive relationship between variables. The relationship was also statistically significant at the .05 level, $t = 3.579$, $p = .009$. For site one, the null hypothesis was rejected and the alternative hypothesis was accepted.

At site two, the teacher ratings for transformational style ranged from 0.65 to 3.90 with a mean rating of 2.27. The site two teacher ratings for principal effectiveness ranged from 0.00 to 4.00 with a mean of 2.20. Appendix D provides the descriptive statistics for leadership style and effectiveness for site two. The Pearson correlation analysis for site two utilized each teacher rater's mean rating for the principal's leadership style and effectiveness to determine the relationship between the two variables and to determine any statistical significance. The inferential analysis revealed a strong positive correlation between the teacher's rating for their principal's leadership style, which was congruent with the principal's self-rating, and the principal's effectiveness ($r = .912$). According to Creswell (2012), an r value between .66 and .85 indicates a strong positive relationship between variables. The relationship was also statistically significant at the .05 level, t = 7.359, p = <.0001. For site two, the null hypothesis was rejected and the alternative hypothesis was accepted.

At site three, the teacher ratings for transformational style ranged from 1.10 to 3.90 with a mean rating of 2.56. The site three teacher ratings for principal effectiveness ranged from 1.50 to 4.00 with a mean of 2.60. Appendix E provides the descriptive statistics for leadership style and effectiveness for site three. The Pearson correlation analysis for site three utilized each teacher rater's mean rating for the principal's leadership style and effectiveness to determine the relationship between the two variables and to determine any statistical significance. The inferential analysis revealed a strong positive correlation between the teacher's rating for their principal's leadership style, which was congruent with the principal's self-rating, and the principal's effectiveness (r=.894). According to Creswell (2012), an r value between .66 and .85 indicates a strong positive relationship between variables. The relationship was also statistically significant at the .05 level, t = 5.969, p = .0002. For site three, the null hypothesis was rejected and the alternative hypothesis was accepted.

All three study sites had a strong positive correlation. A statistically significant relationship between teachers' perceptions of their principal's leadership style and the principal's effectiveness, existed at all three study sites. Therefore, for research question three, the null hypothesis was rejected and the alternative hypothesis was accepted for each of the three study sites. Table 3 provides the correlation analysis results for research question three.

Table 3

Relationship Between Teacher Ratings of Principal's Transformational Leadership Style and Principal Effectiveness

Site	r value	p value
1	.804	.009
2	.912	$< .0001$
3	.894	.0002

EVALUATION OF FINDINGS

The conceptual framework for this study was the relationship between leadership styles and leadership effectiveness. The result for question one was that, at all sites, the teachers indicated agreement and congruency with their principal's self-rating by rating "transformational" as their principal's highest rated style. There was also an indication of teachers' agreement and congruency with their principal's self-rating by rating "transactional" as their principal's second highest rated style at all three study sites. In the same fashion, the teachers' rating of "passive avoidant" was in agreement with their principal's third and lowest self-rated style indicating congruency with their principal's self-rating of passive avoidance.

The result for question two was represented by the mean effectiveness rating values for each of the three sites. An assumption for the study was that the teachers' perceptions of principal effectiveness as measured by the MLQ would be based on overall leadership effectiveness. This is supported by the finding of Eliophotou (2014) that teachers' perceptions of leader effectiveness and teachers' overall job satisfaction were significantly linked to the leadership behaviors in the full range model of leadership.

The result for question three was a strong positive correlation and statistical significance between the study's variables at all three study sites. The inferential analysis revealed a strong positive correlation between the teachers' rating for their principal's leadership style, which was congruent with the principal's self-rating, and the principal's effectiveness level at all the three study sites. This outcome is indicative of the fact that overall, the higher a teacher rated the "transformational" style, the higher their rating was for "effectiveness." This result indicates that teacher ratings of their principal's highest self-rated leadership style can be useful as a predictor for how the teacher will view the principal's effectiveness.

SUMMARY

The MLQ instrument items provided data that were used for descriptive and inferential analyses to arrive at the answers to the research questions for this study. Congruency was found between the principals' self-rated leadership style and the teachers' perceptions of their principal's leadership style. There was a strong positive correlation and statistical significance between the predictor and outcome variables at all three study sites. It was determined that, when there is congruency between principals' perceptions of their highest rated leadership style and their teachers' perception of that style, the teachers' perceptions of the principal's leadership style can be used as a predictor of how the teachers will view principal effectiveness.

Chapter 4

IMPLICATIONS, RECOMMENDATIONS, AND CONCLUSIONS

The problem of interest for this study was that, despite frequent changes of school leadership, elementary schools in the target school district continue to underperform. The purpose of this quantitative correlational study was to investigate the relationship between the congruency of perceived principal leadership style based on the perceptions of principals and teachers and leadership effectiveness. Quantitative method was utilized for this study. The design for the study was correlation. The internal and external validity of the study were threatened by several factors.

Internally, most teachers at the participating sites were reluctant to participate by completing the online survey. For this reason, there is less confidence in the study's results than if there had been a greater rate of participation. One of the study sites had the principal replaced by a new one by the time the proposal of this study could be implemented. At the time of the survey, this new principal had been in the school for about six months as a first time principal and also new to both the school and the teachers. For this reason, a limitation was that the teachers at this site may not have known the behaviors of their new principal well enough to accurately evaluate the principal's leadership style and effectiveness. This limitation connects directly to the study's research problem having to do with frequent changes in school leadership.

Externally, the original proposal for the study called for seven schools to be study sites. However, the researcher was only able to get permission from principals to conduct the study in three school sites. Since the researcher had only three sites with nine teachers at site one, thirteen teachers at site two, and eleven teachers at site three who chose to participate, it is a limit to the extent to which the study's findings can be generalized. The findings are therefore applicable to the three sites and possibly to sites with similar demographics within the target school district. However, the study's findings should only be generalized to other locations with caution and only if the other locations have similar demographics and school profiles.

Prior to gathering data, IRB approval was gained from both The Northcentral University's Institutional Review Board and the New York City Department of Education's Institutional Review Board. Full disclosure of any ethical considerations was included on the first page of the survey in the informed consent document. All the ethical protocols were strictly observed. In the remainder of this chapter, implications, recommendations, and conclusions will be discussed as they relate to the current body of knowledge regarding both leadership styles and leadership effectiveness.

IMPLICATIONS

The first research question for the study asked the following: What is the congruency between principals' perception of their leadership style and teachers' perception of the principals' leadership style in three underperforming elementary schools in an urban New York school district? The result for question one was that, at all three study sites, the teachers indicated agreement and congruency with their principal's self-rating by rating "transformational" as their principal's highest rated style. It has been suggested that leaders fall into one of the three categories of transformational, transactional, or laissez-faire, as measured by the MLQ (Avolio & Bass, 1995).

Transformational leadership style, the highest rated style in the current study, focuses on people. The transformational leader is one that works with the subordinates to achieve a common goal. The transformational leader engages members of his or her team in the decision making process (Avolio & Bass, 1995). This research question one finding has a connection to a study that examined teacher perceptions of transformational leadership qualities among principals. Hauserman and Stick (2013), using data generated from teachers' MLQ responses, found that teachers strongly preferred behaviors that aligned with the aspects of transformational leadership.

Among the three leadership styles of transformational, transactional, and passive avoidant, several studies have revealed high favorability for the transformational leadership style for leadership effectiveness (Balyer, 2012; Day et al., 2016; Hunt & Fitzgerald, 2013; Mokhber et al., 2015; Onorato, 2013). A main concern of every school is to ensure the maximization of all students' academic achievement (Green, 2012, 2013; Gupta & Singh, 2013). The current study's purpose and research problem connect with this information from the literature because at the target sites, leadership styles and leadership effectiveness level of principals, along with frequent changes in principals, seemed to be affecting the effective running of the elementary schools in the targeted school district for this study and student achievement was low. The targeted study sites were selected for two major reasons; underperformance and frequent change of leadership.

Transformational leadership style refers to the ability of the leaders to cater to the needs of their subordinates or followers and subsequently lead them to effective and productive work performance aimed at organizational productivity (Bass & Avolio, 1990). Based on the findings for research question one, the question of why the target sites are underperforming still remains. A possible explanation might reside in the fact that these sites continue to have frequent principal changes. An implication for research question one's findings is that the concept of congruency between principal and teacher perceptions regarding the principal's leadership style may not provide much direction for improving underperforming schools. However, an important implication is that congruency for the concept of leadership style, at least for the leadership style of transformational, does serve as a predictor for teacher perceptions of principal effectiveness.

Research question two asked the following: What is the leadership effectiveness level for principals in three underperforming schools in an urban New York school district? For site one the rating for effectiveness was 2.50, site two was 2.20, and site three was 2.60. This finding was required for answering research question three and aligned with findings in the literature indicating the growing need for effectiveness and efficiency related to leadership to be studied. There is a continuing demand for this type of information from leaders, managers, and administrators of all organizational establishments all over the world (Adeyemo et al., 2015; Al-Omari, 2013; Brauckmann & Pashiardis, 2011; Vermeeren et al., 2014). Similarly, many studies have found that leadership effectiveness is strongly linked to leadership styles, specifically transformational leadership style (Badri-Harun et al., 2016; Cheok & O'Higgins, 2013; Henkel, 2016; Jayakody & Gamage, 2015; Mokhber et al., 2015).

The teachers in this study perceived their leaders to be moderately effective. However, the target schools continue to underperform. An implication for question two's findings is that teacher perception of their principal's effectiveness is not necessarily an indicator of school success. However, the implication remains that congruency between principal and teacher perceptions of leadership style, at least for the leadership style of transformational, does serve as a predictor for teacher perceptions of principal effectiveness, as determined in research question three.

Research question three asked the following: What is the statistical significance, if any, in the relationship between the teachers' perceptions of the principals' self-identified leadership style and leadership effectiveness level in three underperforming schools in an urban New York school district? The null hypothesis for the third research question was there is no statistically significant relationship between the teachers' perceptions of the principals' self-identified leadership style and leadership effectiveness level in three underperforming schools in an urban New York school district. The alternative hypothesis was there is a statistically significant relationship between the teachers' perceptions of the principals' self-identified leadership style and leadership effectiveness level in three underperforming schools in an urban New York school district.

The result for question three showed that all three study sites had a strong positive correlation and statistical significance between the teachers' perceptions of the principals' self-identified leadership style and leadership effectiveness level in three underperforming schools in an urban New York school district. Therefore, for research question three, the null hypothesis was rejected and the alternative hypothesis was accepted for each of the three study sites.

In his study of the relationship between transformational

leadership, perceived leader effectiveness and teachers' job satisfaction, Eliophotou (2014) found that teachers' perceptions of leader effectiveness and teachers' overall job satisfaction were significantly linked to the leadership behaviors in the full range model of leadership.

Furthermore, in a study to expand the understanding of the relationship between transformational leadership and organizational innovation at the organizational level, Mokhber et al. (2015) found that there was a positive impact of transformational leadership on organizational innovation. In their work on how successful leaders combine the practices of transformational and transactional leadership in different ways across different phases of their schools' development in order to progressively shape and layer the improvement culture in improving students' outcomes, Day et al. (2016), supported by Hallinger et al. (2013), concluded that successful leaders combine transformational and transactional leadership to both directly and indirectly achieve their leadership effectiveness.

Even though the question three findings indicated a positive and statistically significant relationship between teachers' perceptions of their principal's highest rated leadership style and principal effectiveness, the targeted schools are underperforming. An implication for research question three's findings is that the positive relationship and statistical significance between teacher perceptions of the principals' self-identified leadership style and leadership effectiveness level may not provide much direction for improving underperforming schools. However, an important implication of this outcome is that information regarding perceptions of leadership style can be used to predict perceptions of effectiveness.

APPLICATIONS FOR SCHOOLS AND ORGANIZATIONS

The problem for this study was that, despite frequent changes of school leadership, elementary schools in the target school district continue to underperform. The results of this study can be used to address this problem in at least two ways. One, the congruency found related to the transformational style of principals is a positive for the schools based on the literature and should be embraced with efforts to maintain consistency in this behavior and more consistency in the tenure of principals at the target schools. Two, the positive relationship between leadership style and effectiveness should be viewed as a positive for the schools. Efforts should be made to build on the positive relationship for the improvement of school performance. Based on the findings in this study, it is recommended that underperforming schools' leaders and leaders of other organizations adopt transformational behaviors in their efforts to have teachers and staff in organizations that perceive the leader's effectiveness in a positive light. It is recommended that the application of these transformational behaviors should be evaluated periodically to ensure that it is yielding a positive outcome as revealed in this study. Leadership style has a direct link to overall job satisfaction and subsequently, to organizational productivity and a reduction in frequent change of leadership (Eliophotou, 2014).

RECOMMENDATIONS FOR FURTHER RESEARCH

The study sample was a sample of convenience that was nonprobability in nature. This nonrandom method of selection did not represent a population with an equal chance of being selected (Baker et al., 2013). It is therefore recommended that further research on the same study topic be carried out with a larger sample that might be more representative of the population. It is also recommended that the study should be done in other levels such as middle school or high school. The study is also recommended to be done at higher performing schools to see if similar results would be obtained. This study could also be done in other types of organizations apart from schools.

CONCLUSIONS

In this quantitative correlational study, congruency of perceptions regarding leadership style, principal effectiveness, and the relationship between teacher perceptions of the principal's highest rated style and leadership effectiveness level at three underperforming schools in a target urban school district in New York were investigated. The predictor variable was teacher perceptions of the congruent style and the outcome variable was the leadership effectiveness level of the principals in the three underperforming schools. This study involved 68 teachers and three principals from three study sites. However, only 33 teachers fully participated in the study by completing the online survey.

After the evaluation of the findings of the data analysis, it can be concluded that, there was congruency between principals and teachers for leadership style. Also, there was a strong positive and statistically significant relationship between the teachers' perceptions of the principals' self-identified leadership style and leadership effectiveness level in three underperforming schools in an urban New York school district. In addition, teacher ratings of their principal's highest self-rated leadership style can be used as a predictor for how the teacher will view the principal's effectiveness. The highest rated leadership style for the principals in this study was transformational.

There is support in the literature for this style as being effective. This information in the literature supports the findings of this study that showed a strong positive and statistically significant relationship between transformational style and effectiveness.

The findings in this study strengthen the current body of knowledge related to the topic of leadership style and leader effectiveness. Finally, leaders in schools and other organizations could use this information in planning for improvement and increased effectiveness.

www.ingramcontent.com/pod-product-compliance
Lightning Source LLC
LaVergne TN
LVHW051841080426
835512LV00018B/3002